T0261330

Building Microservices with ASP.NET Core

*Develop, Test, and Deploy Cross-Platform
Services in the Cloud*

Kevin Hoffman

Beijing · Boston · Farnham · Sebastopol · Tokyo

Building Microservices with ASP.NET Core

by Kevin Hoffman

Copyright © 2017 Kevin Hoffman. All rights reserved.

Printed in the United States of America.

Published by O'Reilly Media, Inc., 1005 Gravenstein Highway North, Sebastopol, CA 95472.

O'Reilly books may be purchased for educational, business, or sales promotional use. Online editions are also available for most titles (*http://oreilly.com/safari*). For more information, contact our corporate/institutional sales department: 800-998-9938 or *corporate@oreilly.com*.

Editors: Nan Barber and Brian Foster	**Indexer:** Wendy Catalano
Production Editor: Shiny Kalapurakkel	**Interior Designer:** David Futato
Copyeditor: Kim Cofer	**Cover Designer:** Karen Montgomery
Proofreader: Rachel Head	**Illustrator:** Rebecca Demarest

September 2017:   First Edition

Revision History for the First Edition

2017-08-31:   First Release

See *http://oreilly.com/catalog/errata.csp?isbn=9781491961735* for release details.

The O'Reilly logo is a registered trademark of O'Reilly Media, Inc. *Building Microservices with ASP.NET Core*, the cover image, and related trade dress are trademarks of O'Reilly Media, Inc.

While the publisher and the author have used good faith efforts to ensure that the information and instructions contained in this work are accurate, the publisher and the author disclaim all responsibility for errors or omissions, including without limitation responsibility for damages resulting from the use of or reliance on this work. Use of the information and instructions contained in this work is at your own risk. If any code samples or other technology this work contains or describes is subject to open source licenses or the intellectual property rights of others, it is your responsibility to ensure that your use thereof complies with such licenses and/or rights.

978-1-491-96173-5

[LSI]

Table of Contents

Preface

The handwriting is on the wall—most people building software and services today are rushing to embrace microservices and their benefits in terms of scale, fault tolerance, and time to market.

This isn't just because it's a shiny new fad. The momentum behind microservices and the concepts driving them is far more important, and those looking for the pendulum to swing back away from the notion of smaller, independently deployed modules will be left behind.

Today, we need to be able to build resilient, elastically scalable applications, and we need to do it rapidly to satisfy the needs of our customers and to keep ahead of our competition.

What You'll Build

Unlike other more reference-style books that are all about showing you each and every API, library, and syntax pattern available to you in a given language, this book is written and meant to be consumed as a guide to building services, with ASP.NET Core simply being the framework in which all the code samples are built.

This book will not teach you every single nuance of low-level C# code; there are far thicker books written by other people if that's what you're looking for. My goal is that by the end of the book, creating, testing, compiling, and deploying microservices in ASP.NET Core will be *muscle memory* for you. You'll develop good, practical habits that will help you rapidly build stable, secure, reliable services.

The mentality I'd like you to have is that after reading this book, you'll have learned a lot about how to build services that are going to be deployed in elastically scalable, high-performance cloud environments. ASP.NET Core in C# is *just one of many* languages and frameworks you can use to build services, but the language does not make the service—*you* do. The care, discipline, and diligence you put into building your services is far more a predictor of their success in production than any one language or tool ever could be.

The paintbrushes and canvas do not make the painting, the painter does. You are a painter of services, and ASP.NET Core is just one brush among many.

In this book, you'll start with the basic building blocks of any service, and then learn how to turn them into more powerful and robust services. You'll connect to databases and other backing services, and use lightweight distributed caches, secure services, and web apps, all while keeping an eye on the ability to continuously deliver immutable release artifacts in the form of Docker images.

Why You're Building Services

Different teams work on different release cadences with different requirements, motivations, and measures of success. Gone are the days of building monoliths that require a custom, handcrafted, artisanal server in order to run properly. Hopefully, gone as well are the days of gathering a hundred people in conference rooms and on dial-in lines to hope and pray for the successful release of a product at 12:01 on a Sunday morning.

Microservices, if done *properly*, can give us the agility and drastically reduced time to market that our companies need in order to survive and thrive in this new world where nearly every vertical, regardless of its domain, seems to need software running in the cloud to make money.

As you progress through the book you'll see the rationalizations for each decision made. From the individual lines of code to the high-level architectural "napkin drawings," I'll discuss the pros and cons of each choice.

What You'll Need to Build Services

First and foremost, you'll need the .NET Core command-line utilities and the appropriate software development kit (SDK) installed. In the first chapter I'll walk you through what you'll need to get that set up.

Next, you're going to need *Docker*. Docker and the container technology that supports it are ubiquitous these days. Regardless of whether you're deploying to Amazon Web Services (AWS), Microsoft Azure, Google Cloud Platform (GCP), or your own infrastructure, Docker provides the portable and immutable release artifacts that you crave (and I'll get more into the details of why this is the case throughout the book).

The development and build pipeline for the services in this book is the creation of Docker images running on Linux infrastructure in the cloud. As such, the path of least friction for readers of this book is likely a Mac or a Linux machine. You'll be able to work with Windows, but some things may be higher-friction or require extra workarounds. The new Linux subsystem for Windows 10 helps with this, but still isn't ideal.

Docker on Windows and the Mac will use virtual machines to host a Linux kernel (required for Docker's container tech), and as such you may find your machine struggling a bit if you don't have enough RAM.

If you're using Linux (I used Ubuntu to verify the code), then you don't need any virtual machines as Docker can run directly on top of a Linux kernel.

Online Resources

- Microsoft's website (*https://www.microsoft.com/net/core/*)
- This book's GitHub repo (*https://github.com/microservices-aspnetcore*)

Conventions Used in This Book

The following typographical conventions are used in this book:

Italic
: Indicates new terms, URLs, email addresses, filenames, and file extensions.

`Constant width`
: Used for program listings, as well as within paragraphs to refer to program elements such as variable or function names, databases, data types, environment variables, statements, and keywords.

`Constant width bold`
: Shows commands or other text that should be typed literally by the user.

`Constant width italic`
: Shows text that should be replaced with user-supplied values or by values determined by context.

This element signifies a tip or suggestion.

This element signifies a general note.

This element indicates a warning or caution.

Using Code Examples

Supplemental material (code examples, exercises, etc.) is available for download at *https://github.com/microservices-aspnetcore*.

This book is here to help you get your job done. In general, if example code is offered with this book, you may use it in your programs and documentation. You do not need to contact us for permission unless you're reproducing a significant portion of the code. For example, writing a program that uses several chunks of code from this book does not require permission. Selling or distributing a CD-ROM of examples from O'Reilly books does require permission. Answering a question by citing this book and quoting example code does not require permission. Incorporating a significant amount of example code from this book into your product's documentation does require permission.

We appreciate, but do not require, attribution. An attribution usually includes the title, author, publisher, and ISBN. For example: *Building Microservices with ASP.NET Core* by Kevin Hoffman (O'Reilly). Copyright 2017 Kevin Hoffman, 978-1-491-96173-5.

If you feel your use of code examples falls outside fair use or the permission given above, feel free to contact us at *permissions@oreilly.com*.

O'Reilly Safari

 *Safari* (formerly Safari Books Online) is a membership-based training and reference platform for enterprise, government, educators, and individuals.

Members have access to thousands of books, training videos, Learning Paths, interactive tutorials, and curated playlists from over 250 publishers, including O'Reilly Media, Harvard Business Review, Prentice Hall Professional, Addison-Wesley Professional, Microsoft Press, Sams, Que, Peachpit Press, Adobe, Focal Press, Cisco Press, John Wiley & Sons, Syngress, Morgan Kaufmann, IBM Redbooks, Packt, Adobe Press, FT Press, Apress, Manning, New Riders, McGraw-Hill, Jones & Bartlett, and Course Technology, among others.

For more information, please visit *http://oreilly.com/safari*.

How to Contact Us

Please address comments and questions concerning this book to the publisher:

O'Reilly Media, Inc.
1005 Gravenstein Highway North
Sebastopol, CA 95472
800-998-9938 (in the United States or Canada)
707-829-0515 (international or local)
707-829-0104 (fax)

We have a web page for this book, where we list errata, examples, and any additional information. You can access this page at *http://oreil.ly/2esotzv*.

To comment or ask technical questions about this book, send email to *bookquestions@oreilly.com*.

For more information about our books, courses, conferences, and news, see our website at *http://www.oreilly.com*.

Find us on Facebook: *http://facebook.com/oreilly*

Follow us on Twitter: *http://twitter.com/oreillymedia*

Watch us on YouTube: *http://www.youtube.com/oreillymedia*

Acknowledgments

This book would not have been possible without the superhuman patience and tolerance of my family. Their support is the only thing that helped take this book from a concept to a published work. I honestly don't know how they put up with my stress and quirks and awful schedule of travel, maintaining my day job, and devoting an absurd amount of hours to this book.

For every chapter and sample in a book like this, there are countless hours of coding, testing, research, consulting with experts, and the mandatory smashing of the head on the desk. I need to thank the open source community at large for their involvement and engagement with .NET Core, especially the advocates and developers at Microsoft.

And as always, I must thank the other members of the A-Team (Dan, Chris, and Tom) for continuing to be a source of inspiration that keeps programming fun and interesting.

CHAPTER 1

ASP.NET Core Primer

.NET Core is not just *yet another .NET version*. It represents a complete overhaul of everything we may have learned as .NET developers. This is a brand new, "1.0" product that is finally going to bring .NET development into the open source community as a fully cross-platform development stack.

This chapter will break down the essential components of ASP.NET Core and .NET Core. In classic Microsoft fashion, there are a dozen new terms and labels to learn, and those have changed multiple times between the betas and release candidates, so the internet is awash with confusing, misleading, or downright incorrect information.

By the end of the chapter, you'll have a better idea of what ASP.NET Core is and how it fits into the new cross-platform framework architecture. You will also have set your workstation up with all of the prerequisites so that you'll be ready to dive into the rest of the book.

Distilling the Core

I'd love to be able to jump straight to the canonical and mandatory "hello world" application using .NET Core. However, Core (I will use ".NET Core" and "Core" interchangeably throughout the book) represents such an enormous shift in architecture, design, and tooling that we need to take a minute to at least cover some of the terminology that has changed from previous versions of .NET.

Even if you've never used .NET before and Core is your first exposure, you'll find this terminology everywhere you search, so knowing what it all means is essential.

CoreCLR

The CoreCLR is a lightweight, cross-platform runtime that provides many of the same features that the Common Language Runtime (CLR) provides on the Windows desktop or server, including:

Garbage collection
> A garbage collector is responsible for the cleanup of unused object references in a managed application. If you've used any of the previous versions of .NET (or Java), then you should be familiar with the concept. Despite the differences between the CLR and CoreCLR, they both follow the same fundamental principles when it comes to garbage collection.

JIT compilation
> As with previous versions of .NET, the Just-in-Time (JIT) compiler is responsible for compiling the Intermediate Language (IL) code in the .NET assemblies into native code on demand. This holds true now for Windows, Linux, and macOS.

Exception handling
> For a number of reasons beyond the scope of this book, exception handling (e.g., try/catch statements) is a part of the runtime and not the base class library.

In the first version of .NET, the CLR was a large, monolithic thing that provided the basic services required by .NET applications. Over time it grew larger and more tightly coupled to Windows. It eventually grew so large that Microsoft had to split the CLR in two, allowing developers to choose full or light versions because the whole thing was usually too bloated for most practical uses. Here, developers generally chose based on whether they were building server or client applications.

With .NET Core, the CoreCLR is now the smallest possible thing that can provide runtime services to .NET Core applications. It is essentially a bootstrapper. Everything not responsible for the most primitive parts of the cross-platform runtime are part of CoreFX (discussed next) or available as completely separate add-on libraries.

CoreFX

People who have been developing .NET applications for some time now should be familiar with the concept of the *base class library* (BCL)—the sum total of all .NET libraries that comprise the framework. If you installed something like ".NET Framework v3.5" on a server, then you would get *every possible class* that came with the framework. This led to developers expecting everything to exist on their servers, and unfortunately to developers treating their servers like pets (more on why this is bad later).

The legacy .NET Framework is an enormous beast, with thousands of classes. When deploying applications to a server, the entire framework has to be installed, regardless of how much of it your application actually uses.

CoreFX (*https://github.com/dotnet/corefx*) is a set of modular assemblies (available as *NuGet packages* and completely open source, available on GitHub) from which you can pick and choose. Your application no longer needs to have every single class library assembly installed on the target server. With CoreFX, you can use only what you need, and in true cloud-native fashion you should *vendor* (bundle) those dependencies with your application and expect nothing of your target deployment environment. The burden of dependency management is now reversed—the server should have nothing to do with it.

This represents an enormous shift in the way people think about .NET development. Building .NET applications is no longer about closed-source, vendor-locked development on Windows. Today, it's a lean, *use-only-what-you-need* model that is absolutely in line with patterns and practices of modern microservice development and how the open source community at large views the art of building software.

.NET Platform Standard

Prior to .NET Core, .NET developers were familiar with the concept of *Portable Class Libraries* (PCLs). These allowed developers to compile their assemblies to target an intersection of architecture and platform (e.g., a Windows Phone 8 DLL and a DLL that could be used by an ASP.NET app on the server). This resulted in multiple different DLLs that were each tagged with where they could be deployed.

The .NET Platform Standard (often just called *.NET Standard*) aims to simplify this process and allow for a more manageable architecture to support .NET Core's cross-platform goals for binary portability. For more information on .NET Standard, check out the documentation on GitHub (*https://github.com/dotnet/standard*).

It may also help to think of .NET Standard in terms of interfaces. You can think of each version of .NET Standard as a collection of interfaces that can either be implemented by the traditional .NET Framework (v.4x–vNext) or by the .NET Core libraries. As you evaluate which NuGet packages you want to use, you'll be looking at which version of the standard they use. If they *don't* conform to some version of .NET Standard, they're not compatible with .NET Core.

Table 1-1 shows the compatibility and equivalencies between .NET Standard, .NET Core, and the existing .NET Framework versions at the time of writing this book (table contains data taken from the official Microsoft documentation (*https://docs.microsoft.com/en-us/dotnet/articles/standard/library*)).

Table 1-1. .NET Standard compatibility

Platform									
netstandard	1.0	1.1	1.2	1.3	1.4	1.5	1.6	2.0
netcoreapp (.NET Core)							1.1	2.0
net (.NET Framework)		4.5	4.5.1	4.6	4.6.1	4.6.2	vNext	4.6.2

ASP.NET Core

ASP.NET Core is a collection of small, modular components that can be plugged into your application to let you build web applications and microservices. Within ASP.NET Core you will find APIs for routing, JSON serialization, and rigging up MVC controllers and views.

Historically, ASP.NET came with the .NET Framework—you could not separate the two. After the split between lightweight and heavyweight frameworks, you could install versions of the .NET Framework that did not include ASP.NET.

Now, much in line with the way the rest of the open source software (OSS) community has been doing things for years, all of the components you need to convert a console app into a web app or service are simply modules you add as dependencies. As with everything that is part of Core, it is 100% open source. You can find all of the source code to ASP.NET Core at *https://github.com/aspnet*.

Installing .NET Core

As mentioned before, you no longer need to install ASP.NET as it is nothing more than a collection of modules from which you can choose to add functionality to your Core app. What you'll need to install is the .NET Core command-line tools as well as an SDK. The distinction between the tooling and the SDK is important, because you can have more than one SDK (e.g., v1.0 and v1.1) installed and managed by a single version of the command-line tools.

This new modular design is a more modern approach to open source frameworks and is exactly how you'll see frameworks for other languages managed and distributed. For folks coming to .NET Core from the OSS world, this should feel natural and second-nature. For developers who have spent a good portion of their careers installing ASP.NET on server after server, this is a new (and hopefully refreshing) experience.

To install .NET Core, simply follow the instructions at the main website (*https://www.microsoft.com/net/core*). Make sure you install the newest version of the SDK (the tooling) *and* the newest version of the runtime.

There are different instructions for each operating system, but when you're done, you should be able to execute the following command without error:

```
$ dotnet --version
1.0.3
```

Your version may vary slightly from the preceding output, but the executable should be in your path and it should produce a version number. This book was written against version 1.0.3 of the SDK and version 1.1.1 of the runtime.

.NET Core has a very active community and a pretty rapid release cycle, so it's quite possible that newer versions of the tooling and runtime will be available by the time you read this.

If this works, then you can be reasonably confident that you've got the basic requirements for .NET Core installed on your workstation. Double-check this with Microsoft's installation instructions to make sure you have the latest version of the tools.

All of the samples in this book assume that your projects will be managed with project files in the form of <project name>.csproj. Note that if you do some basic internet searching for .NET Core samples, you may run into samples that use the project.json file format. These are old and deprecated and not compatible with the 1.x versions of the SDK.

If you ended up with a version of dotnet that is *earlier* than the one shown in the preceding snippet, you may need to download a specific version manually from Git-Hub (*https://github.com/dotnet/core*).

The requirements for this book are that you have a runtime version of 1.1 or greater and an SDK/tools version of 1.0.2 or better.

Tool Versions

Depending on what directory you're in when you run the dotnet command, the version output may vary. If a *global.json* file is a peer or in a parent directory and specifies a fixed SDK version, you will see this version, even if the dotnet command-line tool is a higher version. To see the highest version of the tooling/SDK you have available, run the dotnet --version command from a root or temporary directory that has no nearby *global.json* file.

One side effect of the modularity of .NET Core that many developers may take some time getting used to is the difference between the SDK (tools/CLI) version and the runtime version. The latest runtime version at the time this book was written was 1.1.1. On a Mac, you can use the following command to see which versions of the runtime are available to you:

```
$ ls -F /usr/local/share/dotnet/shared/Microsoft.NETCore.App/
1.0.1/        1.0.3/         1.0.4/
 1.1.0/         1.1.0-preview1-001100-00/ 1.1.1/
```

If you see 1.1.1 in this directory, and you're using 1.0.2 or newer of the SDK, then you should be fine for the rest of this book.

If you do *not* see 1.1.1 in the directory, you're going to want to download it. The list of runtimes is available directly on Microsoft's .NET Core page (*https://www.micro soft.com/net/download/core#/runtime*).

If you're using a Windows machine, you should be able to find your installed runtimes in the following directory: *Program Files\dotnet\shared\Microsoft.NET-Core.App*.

.NET Core is extremely lightweight and, as I mentioned earlier, only includes the bare minimum necessary to get you going. All of the dependencies your applications need are going to be downloaded via the dotnet restore command by examining your project file. This is essential for *cloud-native* application development because having vendored (locally bundled) dependencies is mandatory for deploying immutable artifacts to the cloud, where you should assume virtually nothing about the virtual machine hosting your application.

Building a Console App

Before we can get to any of the really interesting stuff, we need to make sure that we can create and build the world's simplest sample—the oft-derided yet canonical "hello world."

The dotnet command-line tool has an option that will create a bare-bones scaffold for a simple console application. If you type dotnet new without any parameters, it will give you a list of the templates you can use. For this sample, we're going to use console.

Note that this will create project files in the *current directory*. So, make sure you're where you want to be before you run the command:

```
$ dotnet new console

Welcome to .NET Core!
---------------------
Learn more about .NET Core @ https://aka.ms/dotnet-docs.
Use dotnet --help to see available commands or go to
https://aka.ms/dotnet-cli-docs.

Telemetry
---------------
The .NET Core tools collect usage data in order to improve your experience.
The data is anonymous and does not include commandline arguments.
```

```
The data is collected by Microsoft and shared with the community.
You can opt out of telemetry by setting a DOTNET_CLI_TELEMETRY_OPTOUT
environment variable to 1 using your favorite shell.
You can read more about .NET Core tools telemetry @ https://aka.ms/dotnet-cli-
telemetry.

Configuring...
-------------------
A command is running to initially populate your local package cache, to
improve restore speed and enable offline access. This command will take up
to a minute to complete and will only happen once.
Decompressing 100% 2828 ms
Expanding 100% 4047 ms

Created new C# project in /Users/kevin/Code/DotNET/sample.
```

If this isn't your first time using the latest version of the command-line tools you will see far less spam. Worth noting is the telemetry opt-out message. If you're uncomfortable with Microsoft collecting information about your compilation habits anonymously, then go ahead and modify the profile for your favorite shell or terminal to include setting DOTNET_CLI_TELEMETRY_OPTOUT to 1.

Once the project is created, you can type dotnet restore, which analyzes the project dependencies and downloads whatever packages are necessary. This step is required *every* time you modify the project file:

```
$ dotnet restore
  Restoring packages for /Users/kevin/Code/DotNET/sample/sample.csproj...
  Writing lock file to disk. Path: /Users/kevin/Code/DotNET/sample/obj/
  project.assets.json
  Restore completed in 743.6987ms for /Users/kevin/Code/DotNET/sample/
  sample.csproj.

  NuGet Config files used:
      /Users/kevin/.nuget/NuGet/NuGet.Config

  Feeds used:
      https://api.nuget.org/v3/index.json
```

Assuming nothing went wrong, you can now run the application and you'll see the text "Hello World!" emitted to your terminal window (you may experience a delay of a few seconds if this is the first time you've compiled this app to a binary):

```
$ dotnet run

Hello World!
```

Our project consists of two files: the project file (which defaults to *<directory name>.csproj*) and *Program.cs*, listed in Example 1-1.

Example 1-1. Program.cs

```
using System;

namespace ConsoleApplication
{
    class Program
    {
        static void Main(string[] args)
        {
            Console.WriteLine("Hello World!");
        }
    }
}
```

Make sure that you can run all of the dotnet commands and execute the application and see the expected output before continuing. On the surface this looks just like any other console application written for previous versions of .NET. In the next section, we'll start to see immediate differences as we incorporate ASP.NET Core.

If you looked at the *.csproj* file, you might've noticed that it declares which version of netcoreapp it's targeting (1.0).

To make sure that your tools are working properly and your environment is suitable for all of the rest of the code samples in the book (which use v1.1 of the runtime), let's edit this *.csproj* file so that it looks like this:

```
<Project Sdk="Microsoft.NET.Sdk">

  <PropertyGroup>
    <OutputType>Exe</OutputType>
    <TargetFramework>netcoreapp1.1</TargetFramework>
  </PropertyGroup>

</Project>
```

We've upped the NET Core version to 1.1 and changed the dependency on Micro soft.NETCore.App to version 1.1.0. One muscle memory you'll want to start building right away is the need to run dotnet restore after every *.csproj* file change:

```
$ dotnet restore
Restoring packages for /Users/kevin/Code/DotNET/sample/sample.csproj...
Generating MSBuild file /Users/kevin/Code/DotNET/sample/obj/ \
sample.csproj.nuget.g.props.
Writing lock file to disk. Path: /Users/kevin/Code/DotNET/sample/obj/ \
project.assets.json
Restore completed in 904.0985ms for /Users/kevin/Code/DotNET/sample/ \
sample.csproj.

NuGet Config files used:
    /Users/kevin/.nuget/NuGet/NuGet.Config
```

```
Feeds used:
    https://api.nuget.org/v3/index.json
```

Now you should be able to run the application again. There should be no visible change and there should be no problem compiling it.

If you've been following along, take a look at your *bin/Debug* directory. You should see one subdirectory called *netcoreapp1.0* and another one called *netcoreapp1.1*. This is because you built your application for two different target frameworks. If you were to remove the *bin* directory and rerun `restore` and then `run`, you'd only see the *netcoreapp1.1* directory.

Building Your First ASP.NET Core App

Adding ASP.NET Core functionality to a console application is actually quite easy. You could start off with a template from inside Visual Studio, or you could use Yeoman on the Mac to create a new ASP.NET project.

However, I want to show just how small the gap is from a console "hello world" to a web-based "hello world" without using any templates or scaffolding. My opinion is that templates, scaffolding, and wizards should be *useful*, but if your framework *requires* these things then it has too high a complexity burden. One of my favorite rules of thumb is:

> However inconvenient, if you cannot build your entire app with a simple text editor and command-line tools, then you're using the wrong framework.

Adding ASP.NET Packages to the Project

First, we're going to want to add a few package references to our project:

- `Microsoft.AspNetCore.Mvc`
- `Microsoft.AspNetCore.Server.Kestrel`
- `Microsoft.Extensions.Logging` (three different packages)
- `Microsoft.Extensions.Configuration.CommandLine`

Whether you choose to edit the project file on your own or use Visual Studio or VSCode to add the references is up to you.

Throughout the early history of .NET Core, the format of the project file changed. Everything from the initial alphas all the way up through the release candidates and 1.0 general availability made use of a file called *project.json*. During the "preview3" release of v1.0 of the tools, Microsoft created a cross-platform version of the MSBuild tool and embedded that in the command-line tools. As a result, at the time this book went to print, we now have a *<project>.csproj* project file format that works with this new MSBuild.

Here's what our *hellobook.csproj* file looks like with the new dependencies:

```xml
<Project Sdk="Microsoft.NET.Sdk">

  <PropertyGroup>
    <OutputType>Exe</OutputType>
    <TargetFramework>netcoreapp1.1</TargetFramework>
  </PropertyGroup>

  <ItemGroup>
    <PackageReference Include="Microsoft.AspNetCore.Mvc"
      Version="1.1.1" />
    <PackageReference Include="Microsoft.AspNetCore.Server.Kestrel"
      Version="1.1.1"/>
    <PackageReference Include="Microsoft.Extensions.Logging"
      Version="1.1.1"/>
    <PackageReference Include="Microsoft.Extensions.Logging.Console"
      Version="1.1.1"/>
    <PackageReference Include="Microsoft.Extensions.Logging.Debug"
      Version="1.1.1"/>
    <PackageReference
      Include="Microsoft.Extensions.Configuration.CommandLine"
      Version="1.1.1"/>
  </ItemGroup>
</Project>
```

Adding the Kestrel Server

We're going to extend the existing sample so that whenever you issue an HTTP request, you get "Hello, world" in response. We will return that phrase regardless of what URL is requested or what HTTP method is used.

Let's take a look at our new *Program.cs* main entry point, in Example 1-2.

Example 1-2. Program.cs

```csharp
using System;
using Microsoft.AspNetCore.Hosting;
using Microsoft.AspNetCore.Builder;
using Microsoft.Extensions.Configuration;


namespace HelloWorld
{
    class Program
    {
        static void Main(string[] args)
        {
            var config = new ConfigurationBuilder()
                .AddCommandLine(args)
                .Build();
```

```
        var host = new WebHostBuilder()
            .UseKestrel()
            .UseStartup<Startup>()
            .UseConfiguration(config)
            .Build();

        host.Run();
    }
  }
}
```

In this new Main method, the first thing we do is initialize the configuration sub-system. We can use the ConfigurationBuilder to accept configuration settings from JSON files, from environment variables, and, as our sample shows, from the command line. Samples in forthcoming chapters will show more varied use of the configuration system.

Once we've got our configuration built, we then use the WebHostBuilder class to set up our web host. We're not using Internet Information Services (IIS) or the Hostable Web Core (HWC) on Windows. Instead, we're using a cross-platform, bootstrapped web server called *Kestrel*. For ASP.NET Core, even if you deploy to Windows and IIS, you'll still be using the Kestrel server underneath it all.

Adding a Startup Class and Middleware

In classic ASP.NET, we had a *global.asax.cs* file that we could use to accomplish work during the various startup phases of the application. With ASP.NET Core, we can use the UseStartup<> generic method to define a startup class that handles the new startup hooks.

The startup class is expected to be able to support the following methods:

- A *constructor* that takes an IHostingEnvironment variable
- The Configure method, used to configure the HTTP request pipeline and the application
- The ConfigureServices method, used to add scoped services to the system to be made available via dependency injection

As hinted at by the .UseStartup<Startup>() line in Example 1-2, we need to add a Startup class to our project. This class is shown in Example 1-3.

Example 1-3. Startup.cs

```
using Microsoft.AspNetCore.Builder;
using Microsoft.AspNetCore.Hosting;
using Microsoft.Extensions.Logging;
using Microsoft.AspNetCore.Http;

namespace HelloWorld {
  public class Startup
  {
      public Startup(IHostingEnvironment env)
      {
      }

      public void Configure(IApplicationBuilder app,
        IHostingEnvironment env, ILoggerFactory loggerFactory)
      {
        app.Run(async (context) =>
        {
          await context.Response.WriteAsync("Hello, world!");
        });
      }
  }
}
```

The Use method adds *middleware* to the HTTP request processing pipeline. Everything about ASP.NET Core is configurable, modular, and extremely extensible. This is due in large part to the adoption of the middleware pattern, which is embraced by web frameworks for many other languages. Developers who have built web services and applications using other open source frameworks will likely be familiar with the concept of middleware.

ASP.NET Core middleware (*https://docs.asp.net/en/latest/fundamentals/middle ware.html*) components (request processors) are set up as a chain or pipeline and are given a chance to perform their processing in sequence during each request. It is the responsibility of the middleware component to invoke the next component in the sequence or terminate the pipeline if appropriate.

As we've shown in Example 1-3, the simplest possible ASP.NET application has a single middleware component that handles all requests.

Middleware components can be added to request processing using the following three methods:

Map

> Map adds the capability to branch a request pipeline by *mapping* a specific request path to a handler. You can also get even more powerful functionality with the MapWhen method that supports predicate-based branching.

Use

> Use adds a middleware component to the pipeline. The component's code must decide whether to terminate or continue the pipeline.

Run

> The first middleware component added to the pipeline via Run will terminate the pipeline. A component added via Use that doesn't invoke the next component is identical to Run, and will terminate the pipeline.

We'll be playing with middleware components extensively throughout the rest of this book. As I've mentioned, this modular ability to manipulate the HTTP request handling pipeline is key to our ability to make powerful microservices.

Running the App

To run this sample, you can simply type dotnet run from the command line. You should see something very similar to the following when you've run the app. Make sure you've done a dotnet restore prior to this:

```
$ dotnet run
Hosting environment: Production
Content root path:
  /Users/kevin/Code/DotNET/sample/bin/Debug/netcoreapp1.1
Now listening on: http://localhost:5000
Application started. Press Ctrl+C to shut down.
```

You can exercise this service easily using the following terminal commands. Note that any URL you try, as long as it's a valid URL that curl understands, will invoke the middleware and give you a response:

```
$ curl localhost:5000
Hello, world!
$ curl localhost:5000/will/any/url/work?
Hello, world!
```

Out of the box, Windows doesn't come with the curl command. If you have Windows 10 and have enabled the Linux subsystem, then you can use curl from a bash prompt running within Windows. Otherwise, you can just open this URL in a browser or use your favorite REST client testing tool, like the Chrome plug-in Postman.

If you weren't playing the home game and typing the sample as you read the chapter, you can get the full code from the GitHub repo (*https://github.com/microservices-aspnetcore/hellobook*).

Summary

This chapter got you started with .NET Core. You were able to download and install the latest tools (despite the confusing difference between tooling versions and runtime versions), and you created a console app.

We then converted this console application into a simple web application using middleware that responds with "Hello, world!" to all requests. This was easy to do with just a few changes to a project file and adding a few lines of code. Don't worry if not all of the code made sense yet; it'll get much clearer as subsequent chapters go into more detail.

At this point, you should have most of the tools you need for the rest of the book and be ready to dive in!

CHAPTER 2

Delivering Continuously

One of the driving reasons why developers choose to build microservice ecosystems over traditional monoliths is the ability to rapidly deploy enhancements and fixes to small, independently scalable pieces of the system.

This only works if you have confidence that those services are going to work in production before you deploy them.

Introducing Docker

Lately Docker (*https://www.docker.com*) has been gathering momentum and becoming increasingly popular both as a tool to aid development and as one to aid deployment and operations. It is a container tool that utilizes Linux kernel features like *cgroups* and *namespaces* to isolate network, file, and memory resources without incurring the burden of a full, heavyweight virtual machine.[1]

There are countless platforms and frameworks available today that either support or integrate tightly with Docker. You can deploy Docker images to AWS (Amazon Web Services), GCP (Google Cloud Platform), Azure, virtual machines, and combinations of those running orchestration platforms like Kubernetes, Docker Swarm, CoreOS Fleet, Mesosphere Marathon, Cloud Foundry, and many others. The beauty of Docker is that it works in *all* of those environments without changing the container format.[2]

---

1 This is true for real Linux OS hosts. macOS and Windows both require a Linux virtual machine to host the Docker runtime.

2 While the container itself is ubiquitous, some Docker features may or may not be available, depending on the host environment.

As you'll see throughout this book, Docker gives us the ability to create an *immutable release artifact* that will run anywhere, regardless of the target environment. An immutable release means that we can test a Docker image in a lower environment like development or QA and have reasonable confidence that it will perform exactly the same way in production. This confidence is *essential* to being able to embrace continuous delivery.

For more information on Docker, including details on how to create your own Docker files and images and advanced administration, check out the book *Docker: Up & Running* by Karl Matthias and Sean P. Kane (O'Reilly).

Later in this chapter we will demonstrate publishing Docker images to dockerhub directly from our CI[3] tool of choice. All of this will be done online, in the cloud, with virtually no infrastructure installed on your own workstation.

Installing Docker

When installing Docker on a Mac, the preferred method is to install the native Mac application. If you see older documentation referring to something called Boot2Docker or Docker Toolbox, these are deprecated and you should not be installing Docker this way. For details on how to install Docker on your Mac, check out the installation instructions (*https://docs.docker.com/docker-for-mac/install/*) from the Docker website. Instructions are also available for other operating systems, but I won't cover them in depth in this chapter as the online documentation will always be more current than this book.

When I started writing this book, I had Docker version 17.03.0-ce, build 60ccb22 installed. Make sure you check the documentation to ensure you're looking at the newest installation instructions before performing the install.

You can also manually install Docker and all prerequisites via *Homebrew*. It's slightly more involved and, honestly, I can see little use in installing it this way on a Mac. The Docker app comes with a nice icon that sits in your menu bar and automatically manages your environment to allow terminal/shell access.

If you've managed to install Docker properly, it should start up automatically on the Mac. Since Docker relies on features specific to the Linux kernel, you're really starting up a VirtualBox virtual machine that emulates those Linux kernel features in order to start a Docker server daemon.

It may take a few minutes to start Docker, depending on the power of your computer.

---

3 This book will regularly use acronyms like CI (continuous integration) and CD (continuous delivery). It's best to become familiar with these now.

Now you should be able to run all Docker commands in the terminal to examine your installation. One that you'll find you may run quite often is `docker images`. This command lists the Docker images you have stored in your local repository.

Running Docker Images

Now that you can examine the Docker version and the IP address of a running Docker machine, and you can see the list of installed Docker images, it's time to put it to use and run a Docker image.

Docker lets you manually pull images into your local cache from a remote repository like docker hub. However, if you issue a `docker run` command and you haven't already cached that image, you'll see it download in the terminal.

If you run the following command, it will launch our "hello world" web application developed in the previous chapter.[4] It will fetch the Docker image from docker hub if you don't have it, and it will then invoke the Docker image's `start` command. Note that you need to map the port from the inside of the container to the outside port so you can open up a browser from your desktop:

```
$ docker run -p 8080:8080 dotnetcoreservices/hello-world
Unable to find image 'dotnetcoreservices/hello-world:latest' locally
latest: Pulling from dotnetcoreservices/hello-world
693502eb7dfb: Pull complete
081cd4bfd521: Pull complete
5d2dc01312f3: Pull complete
36c0e9895097: Pull complete
3a6b0262adbb: Pull complete
79e416d3fe9d: Pull complete
6b330a5f68f9: Pull complete
Digest: sha256:0d627fea0c79c8ee977f7f4b66c37370085671596743c42f7c47f33e9aa99665
Status: Downloaded newer image for dotnetcoreservices/hello-world:latest
Hosting environment: Production
Content root path: /pipeline/source/app/publish
Now listening on: http://0.0.0.0:8080
Application started. Press Ctrl+C to shut down.
```

The output shows what it looks like after that image has been cached locally. If you're doing this for the first time, you will see a bunch of progress reports indicating that you're downloading the layers of the Docker image. This command maps port 8080 inside the Docker image to port 8080 outside the Docker image.

Docker provides network isolation, so unless you explicitly allow traffic from outside a container to be routed inside the container, the isolation will function just like a

---

4 It's able to do this because we've already published it as a docker hub image. Later in this chapter you'll see how this particular sausage is made.

firewall. Since we've mapped the inside and outside ports, we can now hit port 8080 on *localhost*.

We can see that this application is running with the following Docker command:

```
$ docker ps
CONTAINER ID        IMAGE
COMMAND                 CREATED             STATUS
PORTS                   NAMES
61a68ffc3851        dotnetcoreservices/hello-world
"/pipeline/source/..."  3 minutes ago       Up 2 minutes
0.0.0.0:8080->8080/tcp  priceless_archimedes
```

So let's hit our application with an HTTP client to make sure it's working:

```
$ curl http://localhost:8080/will/it/blend?
Hello, world!
```

This shows that we can download a fully functioning piece of software from docker hub, cache the image locally, and execute the Docker image's run command. Even if we didn't install a single tool for ASP.NET Core or configure our workspace, we could still use this Docker image to launch our sample service. This functionality will be essential to us when we start to run tests in our continuous integration server and need to ensure that the artifact we tested is the *exact* same artifact that we deploy.

The Ctrl-C key combination may not be enough to kill the ASP.NET Core application we're running because we ran it noninteractively. To kill a running Docker process, just find the container ID from the docker ps output and pass it to docker kill:

```
$ docker kill 61a68ffc3851
```

Continuous Integration with Wercker

Depending on your background, you may already have experience with continuous integration servers. Some of the more popular ones in the Microsoft world are Team Foundation Server (TFS) and Octopus, but many developers are also familiar with applications like Team City and Jenkins.

In this part of the chapter, we will be learning about a CI tool called *Wercker (http://wercker.com)*. Wercker and its ilk all attempt to provide a software package that helps developers and operations people embrace CI best practices. This section of the chapter provides a brief overview of CI, and then a walkthrough of setting up Wercker to automatically build an application.

Wikipedia has an excellent section covering the *best practices (https://en.wikipe dia.org/wiki/Continuous_integration#Best_practices)* for continuous integration. I've already discussed some of the *why* for CI/CD, but it essentially boils down to one key mantra:

> If you want more stable, predictable, and reliable releases, then you have to release more often, not less.

In order to release more frequently, in addition to *testing everything*, you need to automate builds and deployments in response to code commits.

Building Services with Wercker

Of all the available choices for cloud-hosted, Docker-based builds I chose Wercker for a number of reasons. First and foremost, *I didn't have to supply a credit card*. Frankly, if a cloud service requires a purchase up front, it might be compensating for a high turnover and departure rate. Free trials, on the other hand, are a marketing bet that you'll like a service enough to keep using it.

Secondly, Wercker is absurdly easy to use, the interface is intuitive, and its tight integration with Docker and support for spinning up multiple attached Docker images for integration testing are outstanding, as you'll see in upcoming chapters.

With Wercker, there are three basic steps to get going, and then you're ready for CI:

1. Create an application in Wercker using the website.
2. Add a *wercker.yml* file to your application's codebase.
3. Choose how to package and where to deploy successful builds.

The first thing you'll need to do before you can create an application in Wercker is to sign up for an account (you can log in with your existing GitHub account). Once you've got an account and you're logged in, click the *Create* link in the top menu. This will bring up a wizard that should look something like the one in Figure 2-1.

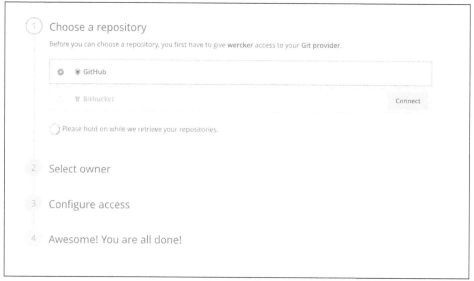

Figure 2-1. Creating an application in Wercker

The wizard will prompt you to choose a GitHub repository as the source for your build. It will then ask you whether you want the owner of this application build to be your personal account or an organization to which you belong. For example, all of the Wercker builds for this book are both public and owned by the *dotnetcoreservices* organization.

Once you've created the application, you need to add a *wercker.yml* file to the repository (we'll get to that shortly). This file contains most of the metadata used to describe and configure your automatic build.

Installing the Wercker CLI

You will want to be able to invoke Wercker builds locally so you can have a reliable prediction of how the cloud-based build is going to go before you push to your Git remote. This is helpful for running integration tests locally as well as being able to start your services locally in interactive mode while still operating inside the Wercker-generated Docker image (again, so you're always using an *immutable* build artifact).

Your code is added to a Docker image specified in your *wercker.yml* file, and then you choose what gets executed and how. To run Wercker builds locally, you'll need the Wercker CLI.

For information on how to install and test the CLI, check out the Wercker developer center documentation (*http://devcenter.wercker.com/docs/home*).

Skip to the section of the documentation entitled "Getting the CLI." Here you will likely be told to use Homebrew to install the Wercker CLI:

```
$ brew tap wercker/wercker
$ brew install wercker-cli
```

If you've installed the CLI properly, you should be able to ask the CLI for the version:

```
$ wercker version
Version: 1.0.643
Compiled at: 2016-10-05 14:38:36 -0400 EDT
Git commit: ba5abdea1726ab111d2c474777254dc3f55732d3
No new version available
```

If you are running an older version of the CLI, you might see something like this, prompting you to automatically update:

```
$ wercker version Version: 1.0.174
Compiled at: 2015-06-24 10:02:21 -0400 EDT Git commit:
ac873bc1c5a8780889fd1454940a0037aec03e2b
A new version is available: 1.0.295 (Compiled at: 2015-10-23T10:19:25Z,
Git commit: db49e30f0968ff400269a5b92f8b36004e3501f1)
Download it from: https://s3.amazonaws.com/downloads.wercker.com/ \
    cli/stable/darwin_amd64/wercker
Would you like update? [yN]
```

If you have trouble performing an automatic update (which happened to me several times), then it's just as easy to rerun the curl command in Wercker's documentation to download the latest CLI.

Adding the wercker.yml Configuration File

Now that you've got an application created via the Wercker website, and you've got the Wercker CLI installed, the next thing to do is create a *wercker.yml* file to define how you want your application built and deployed.

Take a look at the *wercker.yml* file that we use in our "hello world" sample, shown in Example 2-1.

Example 2-1. wercker.yml

```
box: microsoft/dotnet:1.1.1-sdk
no-response-timeout: 10
build:
  steps:
    - script:
        name: restore
        code: |
          dotnet restore
    - script:
        name: build
```

```
          code: |
            dotnet build
      - script:
          name: publish
          code: |
            dotnet publish -o publish
      - script:
          name: copy binary
          code: |
            cp -r . $WERCKER_OUTPUT_DIR/app
            cd $WERCKER_OUTPUT_DIR/app
deploy:
  steps:
    - internal/docker-push:
        username: $USERNAME
        password: $PASSWORD
        repository: dotnetcoreservices/hello-world
        registry: https://registry.hub.docker.com
        entrypoint: "/pipeline/source/app/docker_entrypoint.sh"
```

The box property indicates the base docker hub image that we're going to use as a starting point. Thankfully, Microsoft has already provided an image that has the .NET Core bits in it that we can use for testing and execution. There is a lot more that can be done with *wercker.yml*, and you'll see this file grow as we build progressively more complex applications throughout the book.

We then run the following commands *inside this container*:

1. dotnet restore to restore or download dependencies for the .NET application. For people running this command inside a firewalled enterprise, this step could potentially fail without the right proxy configuration.
2. dotnet build to compile the application.
3. dotnet publish to compile and then create a published, "ready to execute" output directory.

One command that's missing from this is dotnet test. We don't have any tests yet because we don't have any functionality yet. In subsequent chapters, you'll see how to use this command for integration and unit test invocation. After this chapter, every build needs to execute tests in order to be considered successful.

With all of those commands run, we then copy the published output to an environment variable provided by Wercker called WERCKER_OUTPUT_DIR. When Wercker completes a build, the build artifact will have a filesystem that looks exactly as we want it to inside a Docker image.

Assuming we've successfully built our application and copied the output to the right directory, we're ready to deploy to docker hub.

Running a Wercker Build

The easiest way to run a Wercker build is to simply commit code. Once Wercker is configured, your build should start only a few seconds after you push. Obviously, we still want to use the regular `dotnet` command line to build and test our applications locally.

The next step after that is to see how the application builds using the Wercker pipeline (and therefore, within an isolated, portable Docker image). This helps to eliminate the "works on my machine" problem that arises regularly during development projects. We usually have a script with our applications that looks like this to invoke the Wercker build command:

```
rm -rf _builds _steps _projects
wercker build --git-domain github.com \
  --git-owner microservices-aspnetcore \
  --git-repository hello-world
rm -rf _builds _steps _projects
```

This will execute the Wercker build *exactly* as it executes in the cloud, all within the confines of a container image. You'll see a bunch of messages from the Wercker pipeline, including fetching the latest version of the .NET Core Docker image and running all of the steps in our pipeline.

Note that even though the Git information is being specified, the files being used for the local build are the local files, and *not* the files as they exist in GitHub.

You can be reasonably confident that if the build executes locally, it will also execute in the cloud and you know you'll be deploying the same artifact. This is a level of confidence that you cannot get from traditional, non-CI build processes.

It's worth repeating that you didn't have to spend a dime to get access to this CI functionality, *nor* did you have to invest in any of the resources required to perform these builds in the cloud. At this point, there is *no excuse* for not setting up a CI pipeline for all of your GitHub-based projects.

Continuous Integration with CircleCI

Wercker isn't the only tool available to us for CI in the cloud, nor is it the only *free* tool. Where Wercker runs your builds inside a Docker image and produces a Docker image as an artifact output, CircleCI offers control at a slightly lower level.

If you go to *http://circleci.com* you can sign up for free with a new account or log in using your GitHub account.

You can start with one of the available build images (which include macOS for building iOS apps!) and then supply a configuration file telling CircleCI how to build your app.

For a lot of relatively common project types (Node.js, Java, Ruby), CircleCI can do a lot of guesswork and make assumptions about how to build your app.

For .NET Core, it's not quite so obvious, so we need to set up a configuration file to tell CircleCI how to build the app.

Here's a look at the *circle.yml* file for the "hello world" project:

```
machine:
  pre:
    - sudo sh -c 'echo "deb [arch=amd64] https://apt-mo.trafficmanager.net/repos/
    dotnet-release/ trusty main" > /etc/apt/sources.list.d/dotnetdev.list'
    - sudo apt-key adv --keyserver hkp://keyserver.ubuntu.com:80 --recv-keys
    417A0893
    - sudo apt-get update
    - sudo apt-get install dotnet-dev-1.0.1

compile:
  override:
    - dotnet restore
    - dotnet build
    - dotnet publish -o publish

test:
  override:
    - echo "no tests"
```

The key difference between this build and Wercker is that instead of being able to run the build inside an arbitrary Docker image that already has .NET Core installed on it, here we have to use tools like apt-get to install the .NET tools.

You may notice that the list of shell commands executed in the pre phase of the machine configuration is exactly the same set of steps listed on Microsoft's website to install .NET Core on an Ubuntu machine. That's basically what we're doing—installing .NET Core on the Ubuntu build runner provided for us by CircleCI.

CircleCI 2.0 (in beta during the time this was written) is advertising full and native Docker support, so it's possible that by the time you read this the build process will have gotten simpler.

Figure 2-2 shows a piece of the CircleCI dashboard for the "hello world" application.

Whether you decide to use CircleCI, Wercker, or some other CI tool not mentioned in this book, you should definitely look for one with deep and easy-to-use Docker integration. The ubiquity of Docker support in deployment environments and the ability to create and share portable, immutable release artifacts are incredibly beneficial to enabling the kind of agility needed in today's marketplace.

Figure 2-2. CircleCI build history

Deploying to Docker Hub

Once you have a Wercker (or CircleCI) build that is producing a Docker image and all your tests are passing, you can configure it to deploy the artifact anywhere you like. For now, we're going to deploy to docker hub.

We've already seen a hint of how this works in the *wercker.yml* file listed previously. There is a `deploy` section that, when executed, will deploy the build artifact as a docker hub image. We use Wercker environment variables so that we can store our docker hub username and password securely and not check sensitive information into source control.

This deploy step is shown in Example 2-2 to refresh your memory.

Example 2-2. Docker hub deploy in wercker.yml

```
deploy:
  steps:
    - internal/docker-push:
        username: $USERNAME
        password: $PASSWORD
        repository: dotnetcoreservices/hello-world
        registry: https://registry.hub.docker.com
        entrypoint: "/pipeline/source/app/docker_entrypoint.sh"
```

Assuming our docker hub credentials are correct and the Wercker environment variables are set up properly, this will push the build output to docker hub and make the image available for pulling and executing on anyone's machine—including our own target environments.

This automatic push to docker hub is how the sample Docker image you executed earlier in the chapter was published.

In Figure 2-3, you can see a sample Wercker workflow. After we successfully build, we then deploy the artifact by executing the deploy step in the *wercker.yml* file. The docker hub section of this pipeline is easily created by clicking the "+" button in the GUI and giving the name of the YAML section for deployment (in our case it's deploy).

Figure 2-3. Deployment pipelines in Wercker

Summary

We've managed to get through an entire chapter without writing any new code. Ordinarily, something like this would give me the shakes, but it is in service of a worthy cause.

Even if we were the best developers on the planet, and unicorns appeared in the sky floating beneath rainbow parachutes every time we compiled our microservices, we would likely have unreliable products with brittle, unpredictable, error-prone production deployments. We need to be *continuously* building, testing, and deploying our code. Not once per quarter or once per month, but every time we make a change.

In every chapter after this, we will be building microservices with testing and CI in mind. Every commit will trigger a Wercker build that runs unit and integration tests and deploys to docker hub.

Before you continue on to the next chapter, I *strongly* recommend that you take a simple "hello world" ASP.NET Core application and set up a CI build for it on whatever CI host you choose. Put your code in GitHub, commit a change, and watch it go through the build, test, and deploy motions; then verify that the docker hub image works as designed.

This will help build the muscle memory for tasks that should become second nature to you. Hopefully the idea of starting a development project without an automated build pipeline will seem as crazy as the idea of building an unmaintainable monolith.

CHAPTER 3

Building a Microservice with ASP.NET Core

Up to this point in the book we have only been scratching at the surface of the capabilities of .NET Core. In this chapter we're going to expand on the simple "hello world" middleware we've built and create our first microservice.

We'll spend a little time defining what a microservice is (and is not), and discuss concepts like *API First* and *Test-Driven Development*. Then we'll build a sample service that manages teams and team membership.

Microservices Defined

Today, as I have been quoted to say, *we can't swing a dead cat without hitting a microservice.*[1]

The word is everywhere, and unfortunately, it is as overloaded and potentially misleading as the acronym SOA was years ago. Every time we see the word, we're left with questions like, "What is a service, really?" and "Just how micro is micro?" and "Why don't we just call them 'services'?"

These are all great questions that we should be asking. In many cases, the answer is "It depends." However, in my years of building modular and highly scalable applications, I've come up with a definition of *microservice*:

> A microservice is a standalone unit of deployment that supports a specific business goal. It interacts with backing services, and allows interaction through semantically versioned, well-defined APIs. Its defining characteristic is a strict adherence to the Single Responsibility Principle (SRP).

---

[1] Origins of the "can't swing a dead cat" phrase are as morbid as they are plentiful. I have been unable to discover a single credible source for the original quote.

This might seem like a somewhat controversial definition. You'll notice it doesn't mention REST or JSON or XML anywhere. You can have a microservice that interacts with consumers via queues, distributed messaging, or traditional RESTful APIs. The shape and nature of the service's API is *not* the thing that qualifies it as a service or as "micro."

It is a *service* because it, as the name implies, *provides a service*. It is *micro* because it *does one and only one thing*. It's not micro because it consumes a small amount of RAM, or because it consumes a small amount of disk, or because it was handcrafted by artisanal, free-range, grass-fed developers.

The definition also makes a point to mention *semantic versioning*. You cannot continually grow and maintain an organically changing microservice ecosystem without strict adherence to semantic versioning and API compatibility rules. You're welcome to disagree, but consider this: are you building a service that will be deployed to production once, in a vacuum, or building an app that will have dozens of services deployed to production frequently with independent release cycles? If you answered the latter, then you should spend some time considering your API versioning and backward compatibility strategies.

When building a microservice from scratch, ask yourself about the frequency of changes you expect to make to this service and how much of the service might be unrelated to the change (and thus potentially a candidate for being in a separate service).

This brings to mind Sam Newman's golden rule of microservices change:

> Can you make a change to a service and deploy it by itself without changing anything else?
>
> —Sam Newman, *Building Microservices* (*http://shop.oreilly.com/product/ 0636920033158.do*) (O'Reilly)

There's no magic to microservices. In fact, most of us simply consider the current trend toward microservices as just the way Service-Oriented Architecture (SOA) should have been done originally.

The small footprint, easy deployment, and stateless nature of true microservices make them ideal for operating in an elastically scaling cloud environment, which is the focus of this book.

Introducing the Team Service

As fantastic as the typical "hello world" sample might be, it has no practical value whatsoever. More importantly, since we're building our sample with testing in mind, we need real functionality to test. As such, we're going to build a real, semi-useful service that attempts to solve a real problem.

Whether it's sales teams, development teams, support, or any other kind of team, companies with geographically distributed team members often have a difficult time keeping track of those members: their locations, contact information, project assignments, and so forth.

The team service aims to help solve this problem. The service will allow clients to query team lists as well as team members and their details. It should also be possible to add or remove teams and team members.

When designing this service, I tried to think of the many different team visualizations that should be supported by this service, including a map with pins for each team member as well as traditional lists and tables.

In the interest of keeping this sample realistic, individuals should be able to belong to more than one team at a time. If removing a person from a team orphans that person (they're without a team), then that person will be removed. This might not be optimal, but we have to start somewhere and starting with an imperfect solution is far better than waiting for a perfect one.

API First Development

Before we write a single line of code we're going to go through the exercise of defining our service's API. In this section, we'll talk about why *API First* makes sense as a development strategy for teams working on microservices, and then we'll talk about the API for our sample team management service.

Why API First?

If your team is building a "hello world" application that sits in isolation and has no interaction with any other system, then the API First concept isn't going to buy you much.

But in the real world, *especially* when we're deploying all of our services onto a platform that abstracts away our infrastructure (like Kubernetes, AWS, GCP, Cloud Foundry, etc.), even the simplest of services is going to consume other services and will be consumed by services or applications.

Imagine we're building a service used by the services owned and maintained by two other teams. In turn, our service relies upon two more services. Each of the upstream and downstream services is also part of a dependency chain that may or may not be linear. This complexity wasn't a problem back in the day when we would schedule our releases six months out and release *everything* at the same time.

This is not how modern software is built. We're striving for an environment where each of our teams can add features, fix bugs, make enhancements, and deploy to production live without impacting any other services. Ideally we also want to be able to perform this deployment with zero downtime, without even affecting any live consumers of our service.

If the organization is relying on shared code and other sources of tight, internal coupling between these services, then we run the risk of breaking all kinds of things every time we deploy, and we return to the dark days where we faced a production release with the same sense of dread and fear as a zombie apocalypse.

On the other hand, if every team agrees to conform to published, *well-documented* and semantically versioned[2] APIs as a firm contract, then it frees up each team to work on its own release cadence. Following the rules of semantic versioning will allow teams to enhance their APIs without breaking ones already in use by existing consumers.

You may find that adherence to practices like API First is far more important as a foundation to the success of a microservice ecosystem than the technology or code used to construct it.

If you're looking for guidance on the mechanics of documenting and sharing APIs, you might want to check out API Blueprint (*https://apiblueprint.org/*) and websites like Apiary (*https://apiary.io/*). There are innumerable other standards, such as the OpenAPI Specification (formerly known as Swagger), but I tend to favor the simplicity offered by documenting APIs with Markdown. Your mileage may vary, and the more rigid format of the OpenAPI Spec may be more suitable for your needs.

The Team Service API

In general, there is nothing requiring the API for a microservice to be RESTful. The API can be a contract defining message queues and message payload formats, or it can be another form of messaging that might include a technology like Google's Protocol Buffers.[3] The point is that RESTful APIs are just one of many ways in which to expose an API from a service.

That said, we're going to be using RESTful APIs for most (but not all) of the services in this book. Our team service API will expose a root resource called teams. Beneath that we will have resources that allow consumers to query and manipulate the teams themselves as well as to add and remove members of teams.

For the purposes of simplicity in this chapter, there is no security involved, so any consumer can use any resource. Table 3-1 represents our public API (we'll show the JSON payload formats later).

---

2 For more information on semver, check out *http://semver.org/*.

3 Protocol Buffers, or "protobufs" for short, are a platform-neutral, high-performance serialization format documented at *https://developers.google.com/protocol-buffers/*.

Table 3-1. Team service API

Resource	Method	Description
/teams	GET	Gets a list of all teams
/teams/{id}	GET	Gets details for a single team
/teams/{id}/members	GET	Gets members of a team
/teams	POST	Creates a new team
/teams/{id}/members	POST	Adds a member to a team
/teams/{id}	PUT	Updates team properties
/teams/{id}/members/{memberId}	PUT	Updates member properties
/teams/{id}/members/{memberId}	DELETE	Removes a member from the team
/teams/{id}	DELETE	Deletes an entire team

Before settling on a final API design, we could use a website like Apiary to take our API Blueprint documentation and turn it into a functioning stub that we can play with until we're satisfied that the API feels right. This exercise might seem like a waste of time, but we would rather discover ugly smells in an API using an automated tool first rather than discovering them after we've already written a test suite to certify that our (ugly) API works.

For example, we might use a mocking tool like Apiary to eventually discover that there's no way to get to a member's information without first knowing the ID of a team to which she belongs. This might irritate us, or we might be fine with it. The important piece is that this discovery might not have happened until too late if we didn't at least simulate exercising the API for common client use cases.

Test-First Controller Development

In this section of the chapter we're going to build a controller to support our newly defined team API. While the focus of this book is not on TDD and I may choose not to show the code for tests in some chapters, I did want to go through the exercise of building a controller test-first so you can experience this in ASP.NET Core.

To start with, we can copy over a couple of the scaffolding classes we created in the previous chapter to create an empty project. I'm trying to avoid using wizards and IDEs as a starting point to avoid locking people into any one platform that would negate the advantages of Core's cross-platform nature. It is also incredibly valuable to know what the wizards are doing and why. Think of this like the math teacher withholding the "easy way" until you've understood why the "hard way" works.

In classic Test-Driven Development (TDD), we start with a failing test. We then make the test pass by writing *just enough* code to make the light go green. Then we write another failing test, and make that one pass. We repeat the entire process until the list of passing tests includes all of our API design that we've done in the preceding table and we have a test case that asserts the positives and negatives for each of the things the API must support.

We need to write tests that certify that if we send garbage data, we get an HTTP 400 (bad request) back. We need to write tests that certify that all of our controller methods behave as expected in the presence of missing, corrupt, or otherwise invalid data.

One of the key tenets of TDD that a lot of people don't pick up on is that a compilation failure *is a failing test*. If we write a test asserting that our controller returns some piece of data and the controller doesn't yet exist, that's still a failing test. We make that test pass by creating the controller class, and adding a method that returns just enough data to make the test pass. From there, we can continue iterating through expanding the test to go through the fail–pass–repeat cycle.

This cycle relies on very small iterations, but adhering to it and building habits around it can dramatically increase your confidence in your code. Confidence in your code is a key factor in making rapid and automated releases successful.

If you want to learn more about TDD in general, then I highly recommend reading *Test Driven Development* by Kent Beck (Addison-Wesley Professional). The book is old but the concepts outlined within it still hold true today. Further, if you're curious as to the naming conventions used for the tests in this book, they are the same guidelines (*https://github.com/aspnet/Home/wiki/Engineering-guidelines#unit-tests-and-functional-tests*) as those used by the Microsoft engineering team that built ASP.NET Core.

Each of our unit test methods will have three components:

Arrange
  Perform any setup necessary to prepare the test.

Act
  Execute the code under test.

Assert
  Verify the test conditions in order to determine pass/fail.

The "arrange, act, assert" pattern is a pretty common one for organizing the code in unit tests but, like all patterns, is a recommendation and doesn't apply universally.

Our first test is going to be very simple, though as you'll see, it's often the one that takes the most time because we're starting with nothing. This test will be called Query TeamListReturnsCorrectTeams. The first thing this method does is verify that we get *any* result back from the controller. We'll want to verify more than that eventually, but we have to start somewhere, and that's with a failing test.

First, we need a test project. This is going to be a separate module that contains our tests. Per Microsoft convention, if we have an assembly called `Foo`, then the test assembly is called `Foo.Tests`.

In our case, we are building applications for a fictitious company called the *Statler and Waldorf Corporation*. As such, our team service will be in a project called *StatlerWaldorfCorp.TeamService* and the tests will be in *StatlerWaldorfCorp.TeamService.Tests*. If you're curious about the inspiration for this company, it is a combination of the appreciation of cranky old hecklers and the Muppets of the same name (*https:// en.wikipedia.org/wiki/Statler_and_Waldorf*).

To set this up, we'll create a single root directory that will contain both the main project and the test project. The main project will be in *src/StatlerWaldorfCorp.Team-Service* and the test project will be in *test/StatlerWaldorfCorp.TeamService.Tests*. To get started, we're just going to reuse the *Program.cs* and *Startup.cs* boilerplate from the last chapter so that we just have something to compile, so we can add a reference to it from our test module.

To give you an idea of the solution that we're building toward, Example 3-1 is an illustration of the directory structure and the files that we'll be building.

Example 3-1. Eventual project structure for the team service

```
├── src
│   └── StatlerWaldorfCorp.TeamService
│       ├── Models
│       │   ├── Member.cs
│       │   └── Team.cs
│       ├── Program.cs
│       ├── Startup.cs
│       ├── StatlerWaldorfCorp.TeamService.csproj
│       └── TeamsController.cs
└── test
    └── StatlerWaldorfCorp.TeamService.Tests
        ├── StatlerWaldorfCorp.TeamService.Tests.csproj
        └── TeamsControllerTest.cs
```

If you're using the full version of Visual Studio, then creating this project structure is fairly easy to do, as is creating and manipulating the relevant *.csproj* files. A point on which I will continue to harp is that for automation and simplicity, all of this needs to be something you can do with simple text editors and command-line tools.

As such, Example 3-2 contains the XML for the *StatlerWaldorf.TeamService.Tests.csproj* project file. Pay special attention to how the test project references the project under test and how we *do not* have to redeclare dependencies we inherit from the main project.

Example 3-2. StatlerWaldorfCorp.TeamService.Tests.csproj

```xml
<Project Sdk="Microsoft.NET.Sdk">

  <PropertyGroup>
    <OutputType>Exe</OutputType>
    <TargetFramework>netcoreapp1.1</TargetFramework>
  </PropertyGroup>

  <ItemGroup>
    <ProjectReference
      Include
="../../src/StatlerWaldorfCorp.TeamService/StatlerWaldorfCorp.TeamService.csproj"/>
    <PackageReference Include="Microsoft.NET.Test.Sdk"
      Version="15.0.0-preview-20170210-02" />
    <PackageReference Include="xunit"
      Version="2.2.0" />
    <PackageReference Include="xunit.runner.visualstudio"
      Version="2.2.0" />
  </ItemGroup>
</Project>
```

Before we create a controller test and a controller, let's just create a class for the Team model, as in Example 3-3.

Example 3-3. src/StatlerWaldorfCorp.TeamService/Models/Team.cs

```csharp
using System;
using System.Collections.Generic;

namespace StatlerWaldorfCorp.TeamService.Models
{
    public class Team {

        public string Name { get; set; }
        public Guid ID { get; set; }
        public ICollection<Member> Members { get; set; }

        public Team()
        {
            this.Members = new List<Member>();
        }

        public Team(string name) : this()
        {
            this.Name = name;
        }

        public Team(string name, Guid id)  : this(name)
        {
            this.ID = id;
```

```
        }

        public override string ToString() {
            return this.Name;
        }
    }
}
```

Since each team is going to need a collection of Member objects in order to compile, let's create the Member class now as well, as in Example 3-4.

Example 3-4. src/StatlerWaldorfCorp.TeamService/Models/Member.cs

```
using System;

namespace StatlerWaldorfCorp.TeamService.Models
{
    public class Member {
        public Guid ID { get; set; }
        public string FirstName { get; set; }
        public string LastName { get; set; }

        public Member() {
        }

        public Member(Guid id) : this() {
            this.ID = id;
        }

        public Member(string firstName,
          string lastName, Guid id) : this(id) {
            this.FirstName = firstName;
            this.LastName = lastName;
        }

        public override string ToString() {
            return this.LastName;
        }
    }
}
```

In a complete, 100% pure TDD world, we would have created the failing test first and then gone and created all of the things we need to allow it to compile. Since these are just simple model objects, I don't mind skipping a few steps.

Now let's create our first failing test, shown in Example 3-5.

Example 3-5. test/StatlerWaldorfCorp.TeamService.Tests/TeamsControllerTest.cs

```
using Xunit;
using StatlerWaldorfCorp.TeamService.Models;
using System.Collections.Generic;

namespace StatlerWaldorfCorp.TeamService
{
    public class TeamsControllerTest
    {
        TeamsController controller = new TeamsController();

        [Fact]
        public void QueryTeamListReturnsCorrectTeams()
        {
            List<Team> teams = new List<Team>(
                controller.GetAllTeams());
        }
    }
}
```

To see this test fail, open a terminal and cd to the *test/StatlerWaldorf.TeamService.Tests* directory. Then run the following commands:

```
$ dotnet restore
...
$ dotnet test
...
```

The dotnet test command invokes the test runner and executes all discovered tests. We use dotnet restore to make sure that the test runner has all the dependencies and transitive dependencies necessary to build and run. As expected, the test command will fail if either the test code or the project being tested fails to compile.

This test doesn't compile because we're missing the controller we want to test. To make this pass, we're going to need to add a TeamsController to our main project that looks like Example 3-6.

Example 3-6. src/StatlerWaldorfCorp.TeamService/Controllers/TeamsController.cs

```
using System;
using Microsoft.AspNetCore.Hosting;
using Microsoft.AspNetCore.Builder;
using Microsoft.AspNetCore.Mvc;
using System.Collections.Generic;
using System.Linq;
using StatlerWaldorfCorp.TeamService.Models;

namespace StatlerWaldorfCorp.TeamService
{
```

```
public class TeamsController
{
  public TeamsController() {
  }

  [HttpGet]
  public IEnumerable<Team> GetAllTeams()
  {
    return Enumerable.Empty<Team>();
  }
}
}
```

With this first test passing (it just asserts that we can call the method), we want to add a new assertion that we know is going to fail. In this case, we want to check that we get the right number of teams in response. Since we don't (yet) have a mock, we'll come up with an arbitrary number:

```
List<Team> teams = new List<Team>(controller.GetAllTeams());
Assert.Equal(teams.Count, 2);
```

Now let's make this test pass by hardcoding some random nonsense in the controller. A lot of people like to skip this step because they're in a hurry, they're over-caffeinated, or they don't fully appreciate the iterative nature of TDD.

You don't need those kinds of people in your life.

The small iterations of writing just enough code to make a test pass is the part of the discipline that not only makes it work, but builds high confidence levels in tested code. I also find that the practice of writing *just enough* code to make something pass allows me to avoid creating bloated APIs and lets me refine my APIs and interfaces as I test.

Example 3-7 shows the updated `TeamsController` class to support the new test.

Example 3-7. Updated src/StatlerWaldorfCorp.TeamService/Controllers/ TeamsController.cs

```
using System;
using Microsoft.AspNetCore.Hosting;
using Microsoft.AspNetCore.Builder;
using Microsoft.AspNetCore.Mvc;
using System.Collections.Generic;
using System.Linq;
using StatlerWaldorfCorp.TeamService.Models;

namespace StatlerWaldorfCorp.TeamService
{
  public class TeamsController
  {
```

```
    public TeamsController() {
    }

    [HttpGet]
    public IEnumerable<Team> GetAllTeams()
    {
      return new Team[] { new Team("one"), new Team("two") };
    }
  }
}
```

There are very few negative tests we can do for a simple GET method that operates on a collection without parameters, so let's move on to the method for adding a team.

To test this, we're going to query the team list; we'll then invoke a new `CreateTeam` method, and then we're going to query the team list again. Our assertion should be that our new team is in the list.

In the strictest adherence to TDD, we wouldn't preemptively change things unless we did so to make a test pass. However, to keep the listings in the book down to a reasonable size I decided to bypass that. So far, our controller hasn't inherited from a base class, nor has it been returning anything that allows us to control the HTTP response itself (it's been returning raw values).

This isn't going to be sustainable, so we're going to change the way we're defining our controller methods and reflect our *desire* for this new pattern in the failing test shown in Example 3-8.

Example 3-8. TeamsControllerTest.cs—the CreateTeamAddsTeamToList test

```
[Fact]
public async void CreateTeamAddsTeamToList()
{
  TeamsController controller = new TeamsController();
  var teams = (IEnumerable<Team>)
    (await controller.GetAllTeams() as ObjectResult).Value;
  List<Team> original = new List<Team>(teams);

  Team t = new Team("sample");
  var result = await controller.CreateTeam(t);

  var newTeamsRaw =
    (IEnumerable<Team>)
      (await controller.GetAllTeams() as ObjectResult).Value;

  List<Team> newTeams = new List<Team>(newTeamsRaw);
  Assert.Equal(newTeams.Count, original.Count+1);
  var sampleTeam =
    newTeams.FirstOrDefault(
      target => target.Name == "sample");
```

```
    Assert.NotNull(sampleTeam);
  }
```

The code here looks a little rough around the edges, but that's okay for now. While tests are passing, we can refactor both our tests and the code under test.

To make this test pass, we need to create the `CreateTeam` method on the controller. Once we get into the thick of that method, we'll need some way to store teams. In a real-world service, we don't want to do that in memory because that would violate the *stateless* rule for cloud-native services.

However, for testing it's ideal because we can easily manufacture any state we like for testing. So, we'll create the `CreateTeam` method that is a no-op, and we'll see that our test now compiles but fails. To make this pass, we're going to need a *repository*.

Injecting a Mock Repository

We know that we're going to have to get our `CreateTeamAddsTeamToList` test to pass by giving the test suite control over the controller's internal storage. This is typically done through mocks or through injecting fakes, or a combination of both.

I've elided a few of the iterations of test-driven development necessary to get us to the point where we can build an interface to represent the repository and refactor the controller to accept it.

We're now going to create an interface called `ITeamRepository` (shown in Example 3-9), which is the interface that will be used by our tests for a fake and eventually by the service project for a real persistence medium, but we won't code that yet. Remember, we're not going to code anything that doesn't convert a failing test into a passing one.

Example 3-9. src/StatlerWaldorfCorp.TeamService/Persistence/ITeamRepository.cs

```
using System.Collections.Generic;

namespace StatlerWaldorfCorp.TeamService.Persistence
{
  public interface ITeamRepository {
      IEnumerable<Team> GetTeams();
      void AddTeam(Team team);
  }
}
```

We could probably try and predict something more useful than a void return value for `AddTeam`, but right now we don't need to. So let's create an in-memory implementation of this repository interface in the service project, as in Example 3-10.

Example 3-10. src/StatlerWaldorfCorp.TeamService/Persistence/
MemoryTeamRepository.cs

```csharp
using System.Collections.Generic;

namespace StatlerWaldorfCorp.TeamService.Persistence
{
  public class MemoryTeamRepository : ITeamRepository {
    protected static ICollection<Team> teams;

    public MemoryTeamRepository() {
      if(teams == null) {
        teams = new List<Team>();
      }
    }

    public MemoryTeamRepository(ICollection<Team> teams) {
      teams = teams;
    }

    public IEnumerable<Team> GetTeams() {
      return teams;
    }

    public void AddTeam(Team t)
    {
      teams.Add(t);
    }
  }
}
```

If you're cringing at the sight of a static collection as a private member of a class, then that's a *good thing*—you can smell bad code when you're within range. This is, however, code just good enough to make a test pass. If we were intending to use this class for anything other than tests, we'd include multiple rounds of refactoring after we had a complete test suite.

Injecting this interface into our controller is actually quite easy. ASP.NET Core already comes equipped with a scope-aware dependency injection (DI) system. Using this DI system, we're going to add the repository as a *service* in our `Startup` class, as shown in the following snippet:

```csharp
public void ConfigureServices(IServiceCollection services)
{
  services.AddMvc();
  services.AddScoped<ITeamRepository, MemoryTeamRepository>();
}
```

Using the services model, we can now use *constructor injection* in our controllers and ASP.NET Core will automatically add an instance of the repository to any controller that wants it.

We use the AddScoped method because we want the DI subsystem to create a new instance of this repository *for every request*. At this point we don't really know what our actual backing repository is going to be—SQL Server, a document database, or maybe even another microservice. We do know that we want *this* microservice to be stateless, and the best way to do that is to start with per-request repositories and only switch to singletons if we have no other alternative.

Property Versus Constructor Injection

The debate over which method is best will continue raging until long after human beings are even writing code. I prefer constructor injection because it makes the dependencies of a class *explicit*. There's no magic, no detective work involved, and constructor injection is *much* easier to test with mocks and stubs.

Now that we've got a class we can use for our repository, let's modify the controller so that we can inject it by adding a simple constructor parameter:

```
public class TeamsController : Controller
{
    ITeamRepository repository;

    public TeamsController(ITeamRepository repo)
    {
      repository = repo;
    }

    ...

}
```

Note that there are no attributes or annotations required to enable this parameter for dependency injection. This may seem like a triviality, but I've grown quite fond of this fact when working with large codebases.

Now we can modify our existing controller method so that it uses the repository instead of returning hardcoded data:

```
[HttpGet]
public async virtual Task<IActionResult> GetAllTeams()
{
    return this.Ok(repository.GetTeams());
}
```

Next we can make our existing tests pass by going back into our test module and pre-populating the repository with a set of test teams (our tests assume two teams). The test for the collection's getter method will use whatever we supply in the repository so we can make reliable assertions.

It's worth reiterating that our goal with controller tests is to test only the responsibility of the controller. At this point, that means we're *only* testing to make sure that the appropriate methods are being called on the repository. We could have used a mocking framework to avoid creating a custom repository, but the in-memory version is so simple we decided not to incur the overhead of mocking.

Mocking Frameworks

While I don't use mocks much in this book, I have played around with various mocking frameworks available for .NET Core. At the time of this writing my favorite was Moq (*https://github.com/Moq/moq4/wiki/Quickstart*), but feel free to explore on your own to find one that suits your needs.

Just remember the cardinal rule of tools also applies to libraries. They should make your life *easier*, but you should be able to get by without them. If you can't test something without a complicated mock and simple fakes won't do, maybe the class design needs to be refactored.

Completing the Unit Test Suite

I'm not going to bloat the pages in this book by listing every line of code in all of the tests. To finish the unit test suite, we're going to continue with our iterative process of adding a failing test and then writing just enough code to make that test pass.

The source code for the full set of tests can be found in the `master` branch on GitHub (*http://bit.ly/2ukuf82*).

The following is an overview of some of the features of the code enabled through TDD:

- You cannot add members to nonexistent teams.
- You can add a member to an existing team, verified by querying the team details.
- You can remove a member from an existing team, verified by querying team details.
- You cannot remove members from a team to which they don't belong.

One thing you'll note about these tests is that they don't dictate the *internal* manner of persisting teams and their members. Under the current design, the API doesn't allow independent access to people; you have to go through a team. We might want to change that in the future, but for now that's what we're going with because a functioning product can be refactored, whereas a beautiful yet nonexistent product cannot.

To see these tests in action, first build the main source project, then go into the *test/StatlerWaldorfCorp.TeamService.Tests* folder and issue the following commands:

```
$ dotnet restore
...
$ dotnet build
...
$ dotnet test
Build started, please wait...
Build completed.

Test run for /Users/kevin/Code/microservices-aspnetcore/ \
teamservice/test/StatlerWaldorfCorp.TeamService.Tests/bin/Debug/ \
netcoreapp1.1/StatlerWaldorfCorp.TeamService.Tests.dll(
  .NETCoreApp,Version=v1.1)
Microsoft (R) Test Execution Command Line Tool Version 15.0.0.0
Copyright (c) Microsoft Corporation.  All rights reserved.

Starting test execution, please wait...
[xUnit.net 00:00:01.1279308]  Discovering: StatlerWaldorfCorp.TeamService.Tests
[xUnit.net 00:00:01.3207980]  Discovered:  StatlerWaldorfCorp.TeamService.Tests
[xUnit.net 00:00:01.3977448]  Starting:    StatlerWaldorfCorp.TeamService.Tests
[xUnit.net 00:00:01.6546338]  Finished:    StatlerWaldorfCorp.TeamService.Tests

Total tests: 18. Passed: 18. Failed: 0. Skipped: 0.
Test Run Successful.
Test execution time: 2.5591 Seconds
```

Happily, it appears that all 18 of our unit tests have passed!

Creating a CI Pipeline

Having tests is great, but they don't do anyone any good if they aren't run *all the time*, every time someone commits code to a branch. Continuous integration is a key aspect of being able to rapidly deliver new features and fixes, regardless of your team size or geographic makeup.

In the previous chapter, we created a Wercker account and we went through all of the steps necessary to use the Wercker CLI and Docker to automate testing and deploying our applications. It should now be incredibly easy to take our fully unit-tested codebase and set up an automated build pipeline.

Let's take a look at the *wercker.yml* file for the team service, shown in Example 3-11.

Example 3-11. wercker.yml

```yaml
box: microsoft/dotnet:1.1.1-sdk
no-response-timeout: 10
build:
  steps:
    - script:
        name: restore
        cwd: src/StatlerWaldorfCorp.TeamService
        code: |
          dotnet restore
    - script:
        name: build
        cwd: src/StatlerWaldorfCorp.TeamService
        code: |
          dotnet build
    - script:
        name: publish
        cwd: src/StatlerWaldorfCorp.TeamService
        code: |
          dotnet publish -o publish
    - script:
        name: test-restore
        cwd: test/StatlerWaldorfCorp.TeamService.Tests
        code: |
          dotnet restore
    - script:
        name: test-build
        cwd: test/StatlerWaldorfCorp.TeamService.Tests
        code: |
          dotnet build
    - script:
        name: test-run
        cwd: test/StatlerWaldorfCorp.TeamService.Tests
        code: |
          dotnet test
    - script:
        name: copy binary
        cwd: src/StatlerWaldorfCorp.TeamService
        code: |
          cp -r . $WERCKER_OUTPUT_DIR/app
deploy:
  steps:
    - internal/docker-push:
        cwd: $WERCKER_OUTPUT_DIR/app
        username: $USERNAME
        password: $PASSWORD
        repository: dotnetcoreservices/teamservice
        registry: https://registry.hub.docker.com
        entrypoint: "/pipeline/source/app/docker_entrypoint.sh"
```

The first thing to notice is the choice of box in the configuration. This needs to be a docker hub image that already contains the .NET Core command-line tooling. In this case, I chose `microsoft/dotnet:1.1.1-sdk`. This may change depending on which version is the most current as you're reading this, so be sure to check the official Microsoft docker hub repository (*https://hub.docker.com/r/microsoft/dotnet/*) for the latest tags and check the GitHub repository for this book to see what boxes are being used for tests.

In some cases we can skip certain steps and go directly to testing, but if a step is going to fail, we want it to be as small as possible so we can troubleshoot it. You can execute all of these build steps on your development workstation, assuming you have the Wercker CLI installed and a running Docker installation. Just execute the *buildlocal.sh* script that you can find in this chapter's GitHub repository (*https://github.com/microservices-aspnetcore/hello-world*). This script contains the following code and will execute the same build locally that Wercker will execute remotely:

```
rm -rf _builds _steps _projects _cache _temp
wercker build --git-domain github.com \
    --git-owner microservices-aspnetcore \
    --git-repository teamservice
rm -rf _builds _steps _projects _cache _temp
```

Integration Testing

The most official definition of integration testing that I've been able to find indicates that it is the stage of testing when individual components are combined and tested as a group. This phase occurs *after* unit testing and *before* validation (also called acceptance) testing.

There are some subtleties about this definition that are important. Unit tests verify that your modules do what you expect them do. An integration test should not verify that you get the *right* answers from the system; it should verify that all of the components of the system are connected and you get *suitable* responses. In other words, if you're performing complex calculations using components already covered by unit tests, your integration tests need not retest those components. Integration tests would simply verify that you can invoke your web server, trigger the right RESTful endpoint, invoke the complex calculator, and get an appropriate response.

One of the hardest parts of integration testing usually ends up being the technology or code involved in spinning up an instance of the web hosting machinery so that you can send and receive full HTTP messages.

Thankfully, this has already been taken care of for us with the `Microsoft.AspNet Core.TestHost.TestServer` class. We can instantiate one of these and build it with whatever options we like and then use it to create an instance of an `HttpClient` that is preconfigured to talk to our test server. The creation of these two classes is usually done in an integration test's constructor, as shown in this snippet:

```
testServer = new TestServer(new WebHostBuilder()
                    .UseStartup<Startup>());
testClient = testServer.CreateClient();
```

Note that the `Startup` class we're using here is the exact same one we're using in our main service project. This means that the dependency injection setup, configuration sources, and services will all be *exactly* as they would be if we were running the real service.

With the test server and test client in place, we can test various scenarios, like adding a team to the teams collection and querying the results to ensure that it's still there. This gives us a chance to fully exercise the JSON deserialization and use our service the way a completely external consumer might, as shown in Example 3-12.

Example 3-12. test/StatlerWaldorfCorp.TeamService.Tests.Integration/ SimpleIntegrationTests.cs

```
public class SimpleIntegrationTests
{
  private readonly TestServer testServer;
  private readonly HttpClient testClient;

  private readonly Team teamZombie;

  public SimpleIntegrationTests()
  {
      testServer = new TestServer(new WebHostBuilder()
              .UseStartup<Startup>());
      testClient = testServer.CreateClient();

      teamZombie = new Team() {
          ID = Guid.NewGuid(),
          Name = "Zombie"
      };
  }

  [Fact]
  public async void TestTeamPostAndGet()
  {
    StringContent stringContent = new StringContent(
        JsonConvert.SerializeObject(teamZombie),
        UnicodeEncoding.UTF8,
        "application/json");

    HttpResponseMessage postResponse =
        await testClient.PostAsync(
          "/teams",
```

```
            stringContent);
    postResponse.EnsureSuccessStatusCode();

    var getResponse = await testClient.GetAsync("/teams");
    getResponse.EnsureSuccessStatusCode();

    string raw = await getResponse.Content.ReadAsStringAsync();
    List<Team> teams =
        JsonConvert.DeserializeObject<List<Team>>(raw);
    Assert.Equal(1, teams.Count());
    Assert.Equal("Zombie", teams[0].Name);
    Assert.Equal(teamZombie.ID, teams[0].ID);
  }
}
```

Once we're satisfied that this test works properly, we can continue adding more complex scenarios to ensure that various scenarios are supported and working properly.

With our integration tests ready to roll we can update our *wercker.yml* file to execute the integration tests by adding a few script executions:

```
- script:
    name: integration-test-restore
    cwd: test/StatlerWaldorfCorp.TeamService.Tests.Integration
    code: |
      dotnet restore
- script:
    name: integration-test-build
    cwd: test/StatlerWaldorfCorp.TeamService.Tests.Integration
    code: |
      dotnet build
- script:
    name: integration-test-run
    cwd: test/StatlerWaldorfCorp.TeamService.Tests.Integration
    code: |
      dotnet test
```

For such a simple service as this one, it might seem like we've gone to some needless trouble in creating a separate project for our integration tests and using separate CI pipeline build steps.

However, developing habits and practices that you use even on the smallest projects will pay off in the long run. This is one of them. When we get to the stage where we're building services that rely on other services, we're going to want to start up versions of those services while running integration tests. We want the ability to selectively only run unit tests versus integration tests in our pipelines so we can have a "slow build" and a "fast build" if we want. Also, separating the integration tests into their own project gives us a little bit more cleanliness and organization—some of the integration tests I've written in the past have gotten very large, especially when it comes to fabricating test data and expected response JSON payloads for complex services.

Running the Team Service Docker Image

Now that the CI pipeline is working for the team service, it should automatically be deploying a Docker image to docker hub for us. With this Docker image in hand, we can deploy it to Amazon Web Services, Google Cloud Platform, Microsoft Azure, or regular virtual machines. We could orchestrate this image inside Docker Swarm or Kubernetes or push it to Cloud Foundry.

Our options are nearly endless, but they're endless *because* we're using Docker images as deployment artifacts.

Let's run this using a command you should be pretty familiar with by now:

```
$ docker run -p 8080:8080 dotnetcoreservices/teamservice
Unable to find image 'dotnetcoreservices/teamservice:latest' locally
latest: Pulling from dotnetcoreservices/teamservice
693502eb7dfb: Already exists
081cd4bfd521: Already exists
5d2dc01312f3: Already exists
36c0e9895097: Already exists
3a6b0262adbb: Already exists
79e416d3fe9d: Already exists
d96153ed695f: Pull complete
Digest: sha256:fc3ea65afe84c33f5644bbec0976b4d2d9bc943ddba997103dd3fb731f56ca5b
Status: Downloaded newer image for dotnetcoreservices/teamservice:latest
Hosting environment: Production
Content root path: /pipeline/source/app/publish
Now listening on: http://0.0.0.0:8080
Application started. Press Ctrl+C to shut down.
```

With the port mapping in place, we can treat `http://localhost:8080` as the host of our service now. The following `curl` command issues a POST to the `/teams` resource of the service. (If you don't have access to `curl`, I highly recommend the Postman plug-in for Chrome.) Per our test specification, this should return a JSON payload containing the newly created team:

```
$ curl -H "Content-Type:application/json" \
  -X POST -d \
  '{"id":"e52baa63-d511-417e-9e54-7aab04286281", \
  "name":"Team Zombie"}' \
  http://localhost:8080/teams

{"name":"Team Zombie","id":"e52baa63-d511-417e-9e54-7aab04286281",
  "members":[]}
```

Note that the reply in the preceding snippet contains an empty array for the `members` property. To make sure that the service is maintaining state between requests (even if it is doing so with little more than an in-memory list at the moment), we can use the following `curl` command:

```
$ curl http://localhost:8080/teams
  [{"name":"Team Zombie",
   "id":"e52baa63-d511-417e-9e54-7aab04286281",
    "members":[]}]
```

And that's it—we've got a fully functioning team service automatically tested and automatically deployed to docker hub, ready for scheduling in a cloud computing environment in response to every single Git commit.

Summary

In this chapter we took our first step toward building real microservices with ASP.NET Core. We took a look at the definition of a microservice and we discussed the concept of API First and how it is an essential part of building the discipline and habits necessary to allow multiple teams to have independent release cadences.

Finally, we built a sample service in a test-first fashion and looked at some of the tools we have at our disposal for automatically testing, building, and deploying our services.

In the coming chapters, we're going to expand on these skills as we build more complex and powerful services.

CHAPTER 4

Backing Services

In Chapter 3 we built our first microservice with ASP.NET Core. This service exposed some simple endpoints backed by an in-memory repository to provide consumers with the ability to query and manipulate teams and team membership. While it was enough to get started, it's far from an example of a production-grade service.

In this chapter we're going to make our first foray into the world of *microservice ecosystems*. Services never exist in a vacuum, and most of them need to communicate with other services in order to do their jobs. We call these supporting services *backing services*, and we'll explore how to create and consume them by creating a new service and modifying the original team service to communicate with it.

Microservice Ecosystems

As we saw in Chapter 3, it's pretty easy to fire up a quick set of middleware to host some RESTful resources on an HTTP server. These are just implementation details. The *real* work lies in designing ecosystems of microservices, where, within a larger community of interconnected services, each service can have its own release cadence, can be deployed on its own, and can scale horizontally on demand.

To achieve this, we need to put a little thought into what we're doing. While classic "hello world" samples all exist in a vacuum and rely on no other services, we're rarely going to see a lone service in production (with a few exceptions). This was the driving factor behind the discussion of the concept of API First in the previous chapter.

Once we accept the idea that we're going to need multiple services, it becomes far too easy to oversimplify the problem. We assume that we'll have a nice, direct, easy-to-follow dependency chain of services like the one in Figure 4-1.

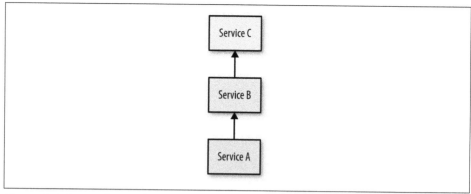

Figure 4-1. An overly simplistic microservice ecosystem

In this completely unrealistic scenario, service A depends on B, which in turn depends on C. With this clear hierarchy in mind, organizations can often make assumptions about processes for developing, deploying, and supporting services like these. These assumptions are dangerous because they can worm their way through an organization until they are no longer assumptions—they've become requirements.

Never assume that there is ever going to be a clear dependency chain or hierarchy of services. Instead, plan for something that looks more like Figure 4-2.

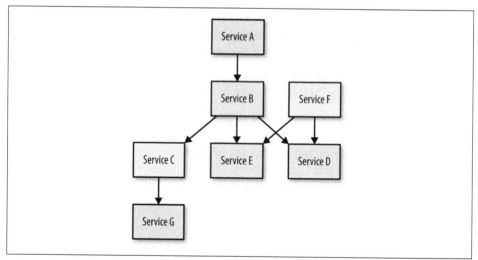

Figure 4-2. A more realistic microservice ecosystem

In this ecosystem, we have a better representation of reality. However, even this diagram is trivial compared to some large enterprises that build and maintain hundreds or even thousands of services. To further complicate things, some of these lines might represent traditional HTTP calls while others might represent asynchronous, Event Sourcing–style communication (discussed in Chapter 6).

Bound Resources

Every application we build needs resources. In the traditional world of deploying apps and services to specific servers (virtual or physical), we're used to our applications needing things like files on disk. These apps also have configuration, credentials, and URLs for accessing other services, and any number of other dependencies that often tightly couple the application to the server on which it is supposed to run.

When we're running our services in the cloud, we need to build our applications with a slightly more abstract notion. Every resource needed by our application should be considered a *bound resource*, and accessed in a way that doesn't violate any of the rules of cloud-native applications.

For example, if our application needs to read and write binary files, we can't assume that we can use `System.IO.File` to read and write bytes to disk. This is because the disk in the cloud must be considered *ephemeral*. It is subject to complete removal without our application knowing. This is part of what allows our services to rapidly and dynamically scale—instances can be brought up and shut down anywhere in the world on demand. If it expects a file to exist on a local disk between requests or process starts, our app is going to fail in unpredictable and potentially catastrophic ways.

The solution is to assume that everything, including the filesystem, is a service. Backing services are *bound* to our application through some mechanism likely facilitated by a cloud provider (PaaS, or Platform as a Service). Instead of opening a file, we communicate with a generalized persistence service. This could be something we build ourselves, or it could be an Amazon Web Services S3 bucket, or it could be any number of other brokered persistence services available.

Likely one of the most common types of bound resources is a database connection. The binding of this resource contains things we should all be familiar with, such as a connection string and credentials. We'll see more about bound resources and database connections in Chapter 5.

Lastly, as we'll see in the samples in this chapter, other microservices are also bound resources. The URLs and credentials to the services on which our own service depends should be considered part of the resource binding.

I should note that the concept of a resource binding is an abstraction, and the implementation of it will vary depending on what cloud platform is hosting your application. These service bindings could just as easily come from environment variables injected by your platform or from an external configuration provider.

Whether you're using Google Cloud Platform, AWS, Azure, Heroku, or just running a bunch of Docker images manually, the key to enabling communications between services is the combination of externalized configuration and treating everything as a bound resource.

Strategies for Sharing Models Between Services

There are a few things that are required for an environment to be considered a microservice ecosystem. The first, obviously, is that you need more than one service. The second is that the services within this ecosystem communicate with each other. Without the latter, you're just standing up an array of isolated and unrelated services.

If we're being diligent about following some cloud-native best practices like API First, then all of our services will have documented, versioned, well-understood public APIs. We might be using a YAML standard like Swagger to document our APIs, or we could be using one based on Markdown, like API Blueprint. The mechanism of defining and documenting our APIs is not nearly as important as the discipline we put into designing our APIs *before* we write our code.

With a well-defined, versioned API that we know isn't going to break out from underneath us, the services within our ecosystem can be built by different teams. Consuming the API from those services then becomes merely a matter of writing simple REST clients.

If it's so simple, then why are we dedicating a section of the chapter to the concept of model sharing? The reason is because as people build ecosystems following the API First rule, once they get into writing the code, they often allow the API boundary to become a *soft* or *blurred* boundary.

Teams frequently make some architectural decisions early on during a project that won't cause trouble until far into the future, when the cost of untangling the mess can get exorbitant.

As an example, let's say that you've got two services in your suite that both operate on invoices. One accepts an invoice from a queue, performs processing, and then submits an updated invoice to another downstream service.

When we look at this solution on paper, it's very easy to say something like, "Let's just extract the invoice model and share it among services." Seems like a great idea, and it's used frequently enough that it is a named pattern, often called the *canonical model* pattern.

Fast-forward a few months, and developers on both service teams have been adding features. The invoice model and its validation rules and (de)serialization code have been factored out into a nice shared module. Because it's easy and gets the job done, both services eventually end up performing their *internal* processing against the *canonical* or *public* model.

Now when one service changes the model in order to accommodate what should be an internal concern, the other service is affected and potentially has builds and tests broken as a result. They've lost the flexibility of true independence, and instead of being a source of flexibility, the canonical model is now a source of tight coupling and is preventing independent team deployment schedules.

It is entirely possible to maintain a canonical model without internal pollution, but you absolutely must be *ruthless* about maintaining a "pure" canonical model and forcing the internals of a service to use an internal model and convert back and forth with an anti-corruption layer (ACL). This is often perceived as a lot of work for little to no benefit, so many teams skip this discipline and lapse into tightly coupling internals to a public model, the consequences of which grow worse exponentially as more and more services adopt this anti-pattern.

Put another way, *two services that are tightly coupled to the same shared internal model are as tightly coupled as if they resided within the same monolith.*

In my opinion, based on years of building new software and untangling the messes of legacy software, the real answer is to *share nothing*. A microservice is an embodiment of the Single Responsibility Principle (SRP) and the Liskov Substitution Principle (LSP). A change to *one* service should never have any impact on any other service. A change to the internal model should be possible without corrupting the service's public API or any external models.

Lastly, before getting into the nuts and bolts of the code for this chapter, I leave you with this quote from Sam Newman about the perils of sharing in microservices:

> The evils of too much coupling between services are far worse than the problems caused by code duplication
>
> —Sam Newman, *Building Microservices*

Building the Location Service

In Chapter 3, we wrote some code as a simplified example of a service designed to manage team information. It allowed for the querying of teams and team members, as well as assignation of members to teams.

We've decided that we also want to maintain and query the locations of all of our team members. We're hoping to eventually build in some map integrations, so as a first step we want to upgrade the team service to contain locations.

But is that really the right way to go? On the surface, it would be really simple to just add a location field to the data store we're using for members. We could probably have that change written in short order.

What happens, however, if we decide in the near future to change how we manage locations without changing how we manage team memberships? Someone could decide they want to convert all of the location data to a graph database. If location and team membership are part of the same microservice, we're violating the SRP and forcing the team service to change every time we modify location management.

It makes more sense to put the responsibility of location management into its own service. This service will manage the location history of individuals (without regard for their team membership). We can add location events to a person, query location history, and as a convenience we can also query for the current location of any individual for whom we have location data.

In keeping with our policy of API and test-first development, Table 4-1 describes the public API for the location service. In our domain, a *member* is a user of the team management application.

Table 4-1. REST API for the location service

Resource	Method	Description
/locations/{memberID}/latest	GET	Retrieves the most current location of a member
/locations/{memberID}	POST	Adds a location record to a member
/locations/{memberID}	GET	Retrieves the location history of a member

If you want to browse the full code for this solution, check it out on GitHub by looking at the no-database branch (*http://bit.ly/2wx6goe*).

First, let's create a model class to hold *location records*, which are records of events in which a team member was "spotted" at a location or his mobile device reported his current location (Example 4-1).

Example 4-1. src/StatlerWaldorfCorp.LocationService/Models/LocationRecord.cs

```
public class LocationRecord {
    public Guid ID { get; set; }
    public float Latitude { get; set; }
    public float Longitude { get; set; }
    public float Altitude { get; set; }
    public long Timestamp { get; set; }
    public Guid MemberID { get; set; }
}
```

Each location record is uniquely identified by a GUID called ID. This record contains a set of coordinates for latitude, longitude, and altitude; the timestamp for when the location event took place; and the GUID of the individual involved (memberID).

Next we need an interface representing the contract for a location repository (Example 4-2). For this chapter our repository is just going to be a simple in-memory system. In the next chapter we'll talk about replacing it with a real database.

Example 4-2. src/StatlerWaldorfCorp.LocationService/Models/ILocationRecordRepository.cs

```
public interface ILocationRecordRepository {
    LocationRecord Add(LocationRecord locationRecord);
    LocationRecord Update(LocationRecord locationRecord);
    LocationRecord Get(Guid memberId, Guid recordId);
    LocationRecord Delete(Guid memberId, Guid recordId);

    LocationRecord GetLatestForMember(Guid memberId);

    ICollection<LocationRecord> AllForMember(Guid memberId);
}
```

Now that we have a model, an interface for a repository, and a repository implementation (it's just a wrapper around a collection, so to save space in the book I left that code on GitHub), we're going to create a controller that exposes this public API. As with all controllers, it is extremely lightweight and defers all of the real work to separately testable components. The code in Example 4-3 illustrates that the controller accepts an ILocationRecordRepository instance via constructor injection.

Example 4-3. src/StatlerWaldorfCorp.LocationService/Controllers/LocationRecordController.cs

```
[Route("locations/{memberId}")]
public class LocationRecordController : Controller {
    private ILocationRecordRepository locationRepository;

    public LocationRecordController(
        ILocationRecordRepository repository) {
        this.locationRepository = repository;
    }

    [HttpPost]
    public IActionResult AddLocation(Guid memberId,
        [FromBody]LocationRecord locationRecord) {

        locationRepository.Add(locationRecord);
        return this.Created(
            $"/locations/{memberId}/{locationRecord.ID}",
```

```
        locationRecord);
    }

    [HttpGet]
    public IActionResult GetLocationsForMember(Guid memberId) {
        return this.Ok(locationRepository.AllForMember(memberId));
    }

    [HttpGet("latest")]
    public IActionResult GetLatestForMember(Guid memberId) {
        return this.Ok(
            locationRepository.GetLatestForMember(memberId));
    }
}
```

Making the repository available for dependency injection is just a matter of adding it as a scoped service during startup, as in Example 4-4.

Example 4-4. Startup.cs

```
public void ConfigureServices(IServiceCollection services)
{
    services.AddScoped<ILocationRecordRepository,
                    InMemoryLocationRecordRepository>();
    services.AddMvc();
}
```

Before moving on to the next section, I suggest you build and test out the location service yourself. Grab the latest code from GitHub (*https://github.com/microservices-aspnetcore/locationservice*) and issue the following commands:

```
$ cd src/StatlerWaldorfCorp.LocationService
$ dotnet restore
...
$ dotnet build
```

Note that the code in GitHub has more than one branch. The code for this chapter contains only an in-memory repository and is under the no-database branch. If you check out the master branch, you'll be peeking ahead at the code for the next chapter.

You can run the application as shown here:

```
$ dotnet run
Hosting environment: Production
Content root path: [...]
Now listening on: http://localhost:5000
Application started. Press Ctrl+C to shut down.
```

With the server running, we can POST a new location record using the following syntax. Note that I've added newlines to this to make it more readable. The curl command you type will all be on a single line:

```
$ curl -H "Content-Type: application/json" -X POST
   -d '{"id": "55bf35ba-deb7-4708-abc2-a21054dbfa13", \
        "latitude": 12.56, "longitude": 45.567, \
        "altitude": 1200, "timestamp" : 1476029596, \
        "memberId": "0edaf3d2-5f5f-4e13-ae27-a7fbea9fccfb" }'
 http://localhost:5000/locations/0edaf3d2-5f5f-4e13-ae27-a7fbea9fccfb

{"id":"55bf35ba-deb7-4708-abc2-a21054dbfa13",
   "latitude":12.56,"longitude":45.567,
   "altitude":1200.0,"timestamp":1476029596,
   "memberID":"0edaf3d2-5f5f-4e13-ae27-a7fbea9fccfb"}
```

We receive back the location record we submitted to indicate that the new record was created. Now we can query the location history for our member (the same memberId we used in the preceding command) with the following command:

```
$ curl http://localhost:5000/locations/0edaf3d2-5f5f-4e13-ae27-a7fbea9fccfb

[
{"id":"55bf35ba-deb7-4708-abc2-a21054dbfa13",
   "latitude":12.56,"longitude":45.567,"altitude":1200.0,
   "timestamp":1476029596,
   "memberID":"0edaf3d2-5f5f-4e13-ae27-a7fbea9fccfb"}
]
```

Satisfied that our location service is working, we can move on to updating the team service.

Enhancing the Team Service

Now that we've created a location service, let's extend the team service we created in the previous chapter. We'll modify the service so that when we query the details for a particular team member, we will also include their most current location and when they were spotted or checked into that location.

To do this, we have two main tasks:

1. Bind the URL for the location service to our team service.
2. Consume the location service once we have the URL.

To see the full implementation of the enhanced team service, check out the location branch (*http://bit.ly/2w6382L*) of the team service repository.

Configuring Service URLs with Environment Variables

As mentioned, there are a number of different ways we can "bind" connection information for backing services to our application. The most important thing for us to remember when doing this is that this information must come from the environment. It cannot be information checked in with our codebase.

The simplest way to do this is to set some reasonable defaults in an *appsettings.json* file, and then allow those defaults to be overridden with environment variables. The defaults are here *only* to make it easier to work on the code from our workstations, and should never be left intact in real environments:

```
{
    "location": {
        "url": "http://localhost:5001"
    }
}
```

With this in place, we can override this setting with an environment variable called LOCATION__URL. Note that there are *two* underscores in this environment variable. Regardless of how the variable was set by the environment, we can query it by checking for the "location:url" configuration setting, thanks to ASP.NET Core's configuration system creating a universal abstraction around the data hierarchy.

We can modify our startup so that we register an HttpLocationClient instance with the appropriate URL (we'll see the implementation of this class shortly):

```
var locationUrl = Configuration.GetSection("location:url").Value;
logger.LogInformation("Using {0} for location service URL.",
    locationUrl);
services.AddSingleton<ILocationClient>(
    new HttpLocationClient(locationUrl));
```

With just a single URL that never changes, this kind of environment-fed configuration is pretty easy. We'll talk about more robust methods of configuring your applications later in the book.

Consuming a RESTful Service

Now that we know how to set up the order of precedence configuration settings allowing our file settings to be overridden with environment variables, we can focus on implementing a location client that talks to our location service.

Since we want to be able to unit test a controller method in our team service without making HTTP calls, we know we're going to start off with creating an interface for our location client (Example 4-5).

Example 4-5. src/StatlerWaldorfCorp.TeamService/LocationClient/ILocationClient.cs

```
public interface ILocationClient
{
    Task<LocationRecord> GetLatestForMember(Guid memberId);
}
```

And Example 4-6 is our implementation of a location client that makes simple HTTP requests. Note that the URL to which this client connects is passed in the constructor we saw in our `Startup` class earlier.

Example 4-6. src/StatlerWaldorfCorp.TeamService/LocationClient/
HttpLocationClient.cs

```
using System;
using System.Net.Http;
using System.Net.Http.Headers;
using System.Threading.Tasks;
using StatlerWaldorfCorp.TeamService.Models;
using Newtonsoft.Json;

namespace StatlerWaldorfCorp.TeamService.LocationClient
{
  public class HttpLocationClient : ILocationClient
  {
    public String URL {get; set;}

    public HttpLocationClient(string url)
    {
        this.URL = url;
    }

    public async Task<LocationRecord>
      GetLatestForMember(Guid memberId)
    {
        LocationRecord locationRecord = null;

        using (var httpClient = new HttpClient())
        {
            httpClient.BaseAddress = new Uri(this.URL);
            httpClient.DefaultRequestHeaders.Accept.Clear();
            httpClient.DefaultRequestHeaders.Accept.Add(
              new MediaTypeWithQualityHeaderValue(
                "application/json"));

            HttpResponseMessage response =
                await httpClient.GetAsync(
                  String.Format("/locations/{0}/latest",
                    memberId));

            if (response.IsSuccessStatusCode) {
              string json =
                await response.Content.ReadAsStringAsync();
              locationRecord =
                JsonConvert
                  .DeserializeObject<LocationRecord>(json);
            }
        }
```

```
        return locationRecord;
      }
    }
  }
```

With a location service client available, we can now modify the controller method in the team service responsible for querying member details. I didn't explicitly cover the code for this controller in the previous chapter, so if you didn't write your own you can find a copy in the GitHub repository (*https://github.com/microservices-aspnetcore/ teamservice*).

We'll modify the controller to invoke the location client so we can append the most recent location for the member to the response (Example 4-7).

Example 4-7. src/StatlerWaldorfCorp.TeamService/Controllers/MembersController.cs

```
[HttpGet]
[Route("/teams/{teamId}/[controller]/{memberId}")]
public async virtual Task<IActionResult>
   GetMember(Guid teamID, Guid memberId)
{
   Team team = repository.GetTeam(teamID);

   if(team == null) {
     return this.NotFound();
   } else {
     var q = team.Members.Where(m => m.ID == memberId);
     if(q.Count() < 1) {
       return this.NotFound();
     } else {
       Member member = (Member)q.First();

       return this.Ok(new LocatedMember {
         ID = member.ID,
         FirstName = member.FirstName,
         LastName = member.LastName,
         LastLocation =
           await this.locationClient.GetLatestForMember(member.ID)
       });
     }
   }
}
```

It's also worth pointing out here that the `LocationRecord` model class we're using is private to the team service. Per the earlier discussion on model sharing, the team service and location service are *not* sharing models, which allows the team service to remain coupled only to the public API of the location service, and not the internal implementation.

We're getting away with what could almost be called an *implicit anti-corruption layer* here because we're using the fact that two JSON payloads look the same on both sides of a conversation.

In more typical scenarios, we would invoke some form of translation utility to convert from the location service's public API format to the type of information we need for our own internal model.

Running the Services

Before we continue, here's a quick recap of what we've done so far. We decided that we wanted to add the ability to maintain a history of location check-ins for each person using our application. To do this, we created a location service that is the sole owner of location data and exposes a convenience endpoint for checking a member's most recent location.

The new location service is in GitHub, in the no-database branch (*http://bit.ly/2w6tLVd*). The team service we modified to consume the location service can be found at the team service's location branch (*http://bit.ly/2w6382L*).

You can also run both of these branches directly from tagged Docker images on docker hub:

- Team service: dotnetcoreservices/teamservice:location
- Location service: dotnetcoreservices/locationservice:nodb

First let's start up the team service. We need to give it two different configuration parameters via environment variables:

- Port number, using the PORT variable. We will have to give our services two different ports if we're running them locally so they don't collide.
- Location URL, using the LOCATION__URL variable (remember, two underscores).

Run the following command:

```
$ docker run -p 5000:5000 -e PORT=5000 \
  -e LOCATION__URL=http://localhost:5001 \
  dotnetcoreservices/teamservice:location
...
info: Startup[0]
      Using http://localhost:5001 for location service URL.
Hosting environment: Production
Content root path: /pipeline/source/app/publish
Now listening on: http://0.0.0.0:5000
Application started. Press Ctrl+C to shut down.
```

Backslashes in Mac Terminal Listings

If you're a Windows user and you're wondering why there are lots of backslashes in the various listings for terminal commands issued at a Mac or Linux command prompt, this is a line continuation character. It lets the user type multiple lines of input, delaying processing until the final carriage return.

This starts the team service on port 5000, maps port 5000 inside the container to port 5000 on *localhost*, and tells the team service that it can find the location service at *http://localhost:5001*.

If you're on a Mac, you can also pass a one-time environment variable straight through to the dotnet run command as shown here:

```
LOCATION__URL=http://localhost:5001 dotnet run
```

With the team service up and running, let's start the location service:

```
$ docker run -p 5001:5001 -e PORT=5001 \
    dotnetcoreservices/locationservice:nodb
...
Status: Downloaded newer image for dotnetcoreservices/locationservice:nodb
starting
Hosting environment: Production
Content root path: /pipeline/source/app/publish
Now listening on: http://0.0.0.0:5001
Application started. Press Ctrl+C to shut down.
```

Now we've got two services running. You can see the Docker configuration for both of those services by using the docker ps command. Next we're going to need to run a series of commands to see everything working:

1. Create a new team.
2. Add a member to that team.
3. Query the team details to see the member.
4. Add a location to that member's location history.
5. Query the member's details from the team service to see their location added to the response.

If you're using Windows, you can achieve the same effect by using your favorite REST client.

Create a new team:

```
$ curl -H "Content-Type:application/json" -X POST -d \
  '{"id":"e52baa63-d511-417e-9e54-7aab04286281", \
     "name":"Team Zombie"}' http://localhost:5000/teams
```

Add a new member by posting to the /teams/{id}/members resource:

```
$ curl -H "Content-Type:application/json" -X POST -d \
 '{"id":"63e7acf8-8fae-42ce-9349-3c8593ac8292", \
   "firstName":"Al", \
   "lastName":"Foo"}' \
 http://localhost:5000/teams/e52baa63-d511-417e-9e54-7aab04286281/members
```

To confirm that everything has worked so far, query the team details resource:

```
$ curl http://localhost:5000/teams/e52baa63-d511-417e-9e54-7aab04286281
```

```
{"name":"Team Zombie",
 "id":"e52baa63-d511-417e-9e54-7aab04286281",
 "members":[{"id":"63e7acf8-8fae-42ce-9349-3c8593ac8292",
   "firstName":"Al","lastName":"Foo"}]}
```

Now that the team service has been properly primed with a new team and a new member, we can add a location to the location service. Note that we *could* have just added an arbitrary location, but the team service wouldn't be able to find it without at least one team with one member with a location record:

```
$ curl -H "Content-Type:application/json" -X POST -d \
 '{"id":"64c3e69f-1580-4b2f-a9ff-2c5f3b8f0e1f", \
   "latitude":12.0,"longitude":12.0,"altitude":10.0, \
   "timestamp":0, \
   "memberId":"63e7acf8-8fae-42ce-9349-3c8593ac8292"}' \
 http://localhost:5001/locations/63e7acf8-8fae-42ce-9349-3c8593ac8292
```

```
{"id":"64c3e69f-1580-4b2f-a9ff-2c5f3b8f0e1f",
 "latitude":12.0,"longitude":12.0,
 "altitude":10.0,"timestamp":0,
 "memberID":"63e7acf8-8fae-42ce-9349-3c8593ac8292"}
```

Finally everything is set up to truly test the integration of both the team and the location service. To do this, we'll query for the member details from the teams/{id}/members/{id} resource:

```
$ curl http://localhost:5000/teams/e52baa63-d511-417e-9e54-7aab04286281 \
 /members/63e7acf8-8fae-42ce-9349-3c8593ac8292
```

```
{
 "lastLocation":
   {"id":"64c3e69f-1580-4b2f-a9ff-2c5f3b8f0e1f",
     "latitude":12.0,"longitude":12.0,
     "altitude":10.0,"timestamp":0,
     "memberID":"63e7acf8-8fae-42ce-9349-3c8593ac8292"},
 "id":"63e7acf8-8fae-42ce-9349-3c8593ac8292",
 "firstName":"Al",
 "lastName":"Foo"
}
```

I apologize for the lack of a shiny interface to these services. This book is all about building services and not about presentation to users. Additionally, given my lack of artistic ability, you really are better off not being subjected to my user interfaces and sticking with `curl` or generic REST clients.

Summary

Microservices are services that do one thing. This implies that services are going to have to talk to each other in order to accomplish multiple things or to join forces to accomplish a "big thing." While there are those who dislike the idea of deploying dozens or hundreds of tiny services, the payoff is worth it when you are able to build, update, and release services independently without affecting others.

In this chapter we talked about some of the complexities of building ecosystems of microservices, and discussed at length some of the technical challenges involved in allowing one service to communicate with another while not violating any of the rules of cloud-native application development.

In the coming chapters, we'll start looking into more complexities and more challenges with microservice ecosystems and discuss patterns and code to solve those problems.

CHAPTER 5

Creating a Data Service

If you've been doing any reading lately about cloud-native services and applications, then you're probably getting sick of hearing that these services all need to be stateless.

Stateless in this case doesn't mean that state can't exist anywhere; it just means that it cannot exist in your application's memory. A truly cloud-native service does not maintain state between requests.

To build stateless services, we really just need to kick the state responsibility a little further down the road. In this chapter, we'll talk about how to build a microservice that depends on an external data source. Our code in this chapter will work with Entity Framework (EF) Core, and we'll upgrade the team and location services we've been working with to true data persistence.

Choosing a Data Store

There are many risks associated with embracing a 1.0-level technology. The ecosystem is generally immature, so support for your favorite things may be lacking or missing entirely. Tooling and integration and overall developer experience are often high-friction. Despite the long and storied history of .NET, .NET Core (and especially the associated tooling) should still be treated like a brand new 1.0 product.

One of things we might run into when trying to pick a data store that is compatible with EF Core is a lack of available providers. While this list will likely have grown by the time you read this, at the time this chapter was written, the following providers were available for EF Core:

- SQL Server
- SQLite
- Postgres

- IBM databases
- MySQL
- SQL Server Lite
- In-memory provider for testing
- Oracle (coming soon)

For databases that aren't inherently compatible with the Entity Framework relational model, like MongoDB, Neo4j, Cassandra, etc., you should be able to find client libraries available that will work with .NET Core. Since most of these databases expose simple RESTful APIs, you should still be able to use them even if you have to write your own client.

For the most up-to-date list of databases available, check the docs (*https://docs.efpro ject.net/en/latest/providers/index.html*).

Because of my desire to keep everything as cross-platform as possible throughout this book, I decided to use Postgres instead of SQL Server to accommodate readers working on Linux or Mac workstations. Postgres is also easily installed on Windows (*https://www.postgresql.org/download/windows/*).

Building a Postgres Repository

In Chapter 3, we created our first microservice. In order to get something running and focus solely on the discipline and code required to stand up a simple service, we used an in-memory repository that didn't amount to much more than a fake that aided us in writing tests.

In this section we're going upgrade our location service to work with Postgres. To do this we're going to create a new repository implementation that encapsulates the PostgreSQL client communication. Before we get to the implementation code, let's revisit the interface for our location repository (Example 5-1).

Example 5-1. ILocationRecordRepository.cs

```
using System;
using System.Collections.Generic;

namespace StatlerWaldorfCorp.LocationService.Models {

    public interface ILocationRecordRepository {
        LocationRecord Add(LocationRecord locationRecord);
        LocationRecord Update(LocationRecord locationRecord);
        LocationRecord Get(Guid memberId, Guid recordId);
        LocationRecord Delete(Guid memberId, Guid recordId);

        LocationRecord GetLatestForMember(Guid memberId);
```

```
        ICollection<LocationRecord> AllForMember(Guid memberId);
    }
}
```

The location repository exposes standard CRUD functions like Add, Update, Get, and Delete. In addition, this repository exposes methods to obtain the latest location entry for a member as well as the entire location history for a member.

The purpose of the location service is solely to track location data, so you'll notice that there is no reference to team membership at all in this interface.

Creating a Database Context

The next thing we're going to do is create a *database context*. This class will serve as a wrapper around the base DbContext class we get from Entity Framework Core. Since we're dealing with locations, we'll call our context class LocationDbContext.

If you're not familiar with Entity Framework or EF Core, the database context acts as the gateway between your database-agnostic model class (POCOs, or Plain-Old C# Objects) and the real database. For more information on EF Core, check out Microsoft's documentation (*https://docs.microsoft.com/en-us/ef/core/*). We could probably spend another several chapters doing nothing but exploring its details, but since we're trying to stay focused on cloud-native applications and services, we'll use just enough EF Core to build our services.

The pattern for using a database context is to create a class that inherits from it that is specific to your model. In our case, since we're dealing with locations, we'll create a LocationDbContext class (Example 5-2).

Example 5-2. LocationDbContext.cs

```
using Microsoft.EntityFrameworkCore;
using StatlerWaldorfCorp.LocationService.Models;
using Npgsql.EntityFrameworkCore.PostgreSQL;

namespace StatlerWaldorfCorp.LocationService.Persistence
{
    public class LocationDbContext : DbContext
    {
      public LocationDbContext(
        DbContextOptions<LocationDbContext> options) :
          base(options)
      {
      }

      protected override void OnModelCreating(
        ModelBuilder modelBuilder)
      {
```

```
        base.OnModelCreating(modelBuilder);
        modelBuilder.HasPostgresExtension("uuid-ossp");
    }

    public DbSet<LocationRecord> LocationRecords {get; set;}
  }
}
```

Here we can use the ModelBuilder and DbContextOptions classes to perform any additional setup we need on the context. In our case, we're ensuring that our model has the uuid-ossp Postgres extension to support the member ID field.

Implementing the Location Record Repository Interface

Now that we have a context through which other classes can use to communicate with the database, we can create a real implementation of the ILocationRecordRepository interface. This real implementation will take an instance of LocationDbContext as a constructor parameter. This sets us up nicely to configure this context with environment-supplied connection strings when deploying for real and with mocks or in-memory providers (discussed later) when testing.

Example 5-3 contains the code for the LocationRecordRepository class.

Example 5-3. LocationRecordRepository.cs

```
using System;
using System.Linq;
using System.Collections.Generic;
using StatlerWaldorfCorp.LocationService.Models;

namespace StatlerWaldorfCorp.LocationService.Persistence
{
  public class LocationRecordRepository :
    ILocationRecordRepository
  {
      private LocationDbContext context;

      public LocationRecordRepository(LocationDbContext context)
      {
          this.context = context;
      }

      public LocationRecord Add(LocationRecord locationRecord)
      {
          this.context.Add(locationRecord);
          this.context.SaveChanges();
          return locationRecord;
      }
```

```
public LocationRecord Update(LocationRecord locationRecord)
{
    this.context.Entry(locationRecord).State =
        EntityState.Modified;
    this.context.SaveChanges();
    return locationRecord;
}

public LocationRecord Get(Guid memberId, Guid recordId)
{
    return this.context.LocationRecords
      .Single(lr => lr.MemberID == memberId &&
                    lr.ID == recordId);
}

public LocationRecord Delete(Guid memberId, Guid recordId)
{
    LocationRecord locationRecord =
      this.Get(memberId, recordId);
    this.context.Remove(locationRecord);
    this.context.SaveChanges();
    return locationRecord;
}

public LocationRecord GetLatestForMember(Guid memberId)
{
    LocationRecord locationRecord =
      this.context.LocationRecords.
        Where(lr => lr.MemberID == memberId).
        OrderBy(lr => lr.Timestamp).
        Last();
    return locationRecord;
}

public ICollection<LocationRecord> AllForMember(Guid memberId)
{
    return this.context.LocationRecords.
        Where(lr => lr.MemberID == memberId).
        OrderBy(lr => lr.Timestamp).
        ToList();
}
    }
}
```

The code here is pretty straightforward. Any time we make a change to the database, we call SaveChanges on the context. If we need to query, we use the LINQ expression syntax where we can combine Where and OrderBy to filter and sort the results.

When we do an update, we need to flag the entity we're updating as a modified entry so that Entity Framework Core knows how to generate an appropriate SQL UPDATE statement for that record. If we don't modify this entry state, EF Core won't know anything has changed and so a call to SaveChanges will do nothing.

The next big trick in this repository is injecting the Postgres-specific database context. To make this happen, we need to add this repository to the dependency injection system in the ConfigureServices method of our Startup class (Example 5-4).

Example 5-4. ConfigureServices method in Startup.cs

```
public void ConfigureServices(IServiceCollection services)
{
    services.AddEntityFrameworkNpgsql()
        .AddDbContext<LocationDbContext>(options =>
            options.UseNpgsql(Configuration));
    services.AddScoped<ILocationRecordRepository,
        LocationRecordRepository>();
    services.AddMvc();
}
```

First we want to use the AddEntityFrameworkNpgsql extension method exposed by the Postgres EF Core provider. Next, we add our location repository as a scoped service. When we use the AddScoped method, we're indicating that every new request made to our service gets a newly created instance of this repository.

Testing with the Entity Framework Core In-Memory Provider

So far we've created an interface that represents the contract to which our repositories must conform. We've got an in-memory implementation of a repository and we've got a repository that wraps a DbContext configured to talk to PostgreSQL.

You might be wondering how (or if) we can test the database context wrapper in isolation, since we can already test the repository in isolation. Microsoft does have an in-memory provider (*http://bit.ly/2wm0ntt*) for Entity Framework Core. There are a couple of drawbacks to this provider, however. First and foremost, the InMemory provider is *not* a relational database. This means that you can save data using this provider that might normally violate a real database's referential integrity and foreign key constraints.

If you dig a little deeper into this provider, you'll realize that it is essentially an EF Core facade around simple in-memory collection storage. We have already built a repository that works against collection objects, so the only added value this provider gives us is a little bit of additional code coverage to ensure that our database context is actually invoked. You should *not* assume that the InMemory provider is going to give you confidence that your database operations will behave as planned.

It is for these reasons, and the fact that this is not a book focused on TDD, that I decided to skip writing tests using this provider. We've got unit tests for our repositories and, as you'll see later in the chapter, we're going to be building automated integration tests that talk to a real PostgreSQL database.

I'll leave it up to you to decide whether you think the use of the InMemory provider will add testing value and confidence to your projects.

Databases Are Backing Services

When we talk about making our services *cloud native*, one of the things that always comes up is the notion of backing services. Put simply, this means that we need to treat everything that our application needs to function as a bound resource: files, databases, services, messaging, etc.

Every backing service our application needs should be configurable externally. As such, we need to be able to get our database connection string from someplace *other* than our code. If we check a connection string into source control, then we've already violated some of the cardinal rules of cloud-native application development.

The means by which an application gets its external configuration vary from platform to platform. For this sample we're going to use environment variables that can override defaults supplied by a configuration file.

This *appsettings.json* file looks like the one here (newlines inside the connection string are for book formatting only):

```
{
    "transient": false,
    "postgres": {
        "cstr": "Host=localhost;Port=5432;Database=locationservice;
Username=integrator;Password=inteword"
    }
}
```

This scenario makes it very easy to override default configuration in deployment environments but have a relatively low-friction developer experience on our development workstations.

Configuring a Postgres Database Context

The repository we built earlier requires some kind of database context in order to function. The database context is the core primitive of Entity Framework Core. (This book is not an EF Core reference manual, so if you want additional information you should consult the official documentation.)

To create a database context for the location model, we just need to create a class that inherits from DbContext. I've also included a DbContextFactory because that can sometimes make running the Entity Framework Core command-line tools simpler:

```
using Microsoft.EntityFrameworkCore;
using Microsoft.EntityFrameworkCore.Infrastructure;
using StatlerWaldorfCorp.LocationService.Models;
using Npgsql.EntityFrameworkCore.PostgreSQL;

namespace StatlerWaldorfCorp.LocationService.Persistence
{
    public class LocationDbContext : DbContext
    {
        public LocationDbContext(
          DbContextOptions<LocationDbContext> options) :base(options)
        {
        }

        protected override void OnModelCreating(
            ModelBuilder modelBuilder)
        {
            base.OnModelCreating(modelBuilder);
            modelBuilder.HasPostgresExtension("uuid-ossp");
        }

        public DbSet<LocationRecord> LocationRecords {get; set;}
    }

    public class LocationDbContextFactory :
     IDbContextFactory<LocationDbContext>
    {
        public LocationDbContext
          Create(DbContextFactoryOptions options)
        {
            var optionsBuilder =
              new DbContextOptionsBuilder<LocationDbContext>();
            var connectionString =
              Startup.Configuration
                .GetSection("postgres:cstr").Value;
            optionsBuilder.UseNpgsql(connectionString);

            return new LocationDbContext(optionsBuilder.Options);
        }
    }
}
```

With a new database context, we need to make it available for dependency injection so that the location repository can utilize it:

```
public void ConfigureServices(IServiceCollection services)
{
    var transient = true;
    if (Configuration.GetSection("transient") != null) {
        transient = Boolean.Parse(Configuration
          .GetSection("transient").Value);
    }
    if (transient) {
        logger.LogInformation(
          "Using transient location record repository.");
        services.AddScoped<ILocationRecordRepository,
                        InMemoryLocationRecordRepository>();
    } else {
        var connectionString =
          Configuration.GetSection("postgres:cstr").Value;
        services.AddEntityFrameworkNpgsql()
              .AddDbContext<LocationDbContext>(options =>
                    options.UseNpgsql(connectionString));
        logger.LogInformation(
          "Using '{0}' for DB connection string.",
          connectionString);
        services.AddScoped<ILocationRecordRepository,
          LocationRecordRepository>();
    }

    services.AddMvc();
}
```

The calls to AddEntityFrameworkNpgsql and AddDbContext are the magic that makes everything happen here.

With a context configured for DI, our service should be ready to run, test, and accept EF Core command-line parameters like the ones we need to execute migrations. You can see the code for the migrations in the location service's GitHub repository (*https://github.com/microservices-aspnetcore/locationservice*). When building your own database-backed services, you can also use the EF Core command-line tools to reverse-engineer migrations from existing database schemas.

Integration Testing Real Repositories

We've unit tested all of our code, and we've made the decision to not use the InMemory EF Core data provider, but we still don't have full confidence in our service. The only way we're going to have full confidence is when we exercise our repository class against a real Postgres database.

Back in the old days, when developers rode dinosaurs to and from the office, we would have installed Postgres on our local workstation, configured it manually, and even manually triggered a test that would exercise the repository class against this local instance.

This pattern is the *antithesis* of the kind of agility and automation we want when building applications for the cloud. No, what we want instead is for our automated build pipeline to spin up a fresh, empty instance of Postgres *every time* we run the build. Then we want integration tests to run against this fresh instance, including running our migrations to set up the schema in the database. We want this to work locally, on our teammates' workstations, and in the cloud, all automatically after every commit.

This is why I enjoy the combination of Wercker and Docker (though most Docker-native CI tools support similar functionality). If we just add the following lines to the top of our *wercker.yml* file, the Wercker CLI (and the hosted version in the cloud) will spin up a connected Postgres Docker image and create a bunch of environment variables that provide the host IP, port, and credentials for the database (Example 5-5).

Example 5-5. Declaring a backing service for a Wercker build in wercker.yml

```
services:
  - id: postgres
    env:
      POSTGRES_PASSWORD: inteword
      POSTGRES_USER: integrator
      POSTGRES_DB: locationservice
```

We can specify the credentials we're going to use or we can let Wercker pick them. Either way, the credentials and other relevant information are made available to our build pipeline in environment variables.

Normally we would throw a fit about checking in credentials, but since these credentials are only used to configure a short-lived database that only exists long enough to run integration tests inside a private container, this isn't dangerous. If these credentials pointed to a database that existed anywhere in a semi-permanent environment, that would be a red flag.

Line Wraps in Code Listings

This chapter has a lot of connection strings that wrap across lines in the printed and electronic book. These line wraps don't exist in the actual YAML, JSON, or C# files. Please double-check with the files in GitHub if you're not sure when there should or should not be a line feed.

Now we can set up some build steps that prepare for and execute integration tests, as in Example 5-6.

Example 5-6. Integration testing in a Wercker build

```
# integration tests
    - script:
        name: integration-migrate
        cwd: src/StatlerWaldorfCorp.LocationService
        code: |
            export TRANSIENT=false
            export POSTGRES__CSTR=
"Host=$POSTGRES_PORT_5432_TCP_ADDR"
            export POSTGRES__CSTR=
"$POSTGRES__CSTR;Username=integrator;Password=inteword;"
            export POSTGRES__CSTR=
"$POSTGRES__CSTR;Port=$POSTGRES_PORT_5432_TCP_PORT;
  Database=locationservice"
            dotnet ef database update
    - script:
        name: integration-restore
        cwd: test/StatlerWaldorfCorp.LocationService.Integration
        code: |
            dotnet restore
    - script:
        name: integration-build
        cwd: test/StatlerWaldorfCorp.LocationService.Integration
        code: |
          dotnet build
    - script:
        name: integration-test
        cwd: test/StatlerWaldorfCorp.LocationService.Integration
        code: |
          dotnet test
```

The awkward-looking concatenation of the shell variable is just a way of making it slightly clearer how that variable is being created, and sometimes you run into parsing issues with the semicolons that cut off the rest of the environment variable.

The following is the list of commands being executed by the integration suite:

`dotnet ef database update`
Ensures that the schema in the database matches what our EF Core model expects. This will actually instantiate the `Startup` class, call `ConfigureServices`, and attempt to pluck out the `LocationDbContext` class and then execute the migrations stored in the project.

`dotnet restore`
Verifies and collects dependencies for our integration test project.

`dotnet build`
Compiles our integration test project.

```
dotnet test
```
Runs the detected tests in our integration test project.

You can see the full *wercker.yml* file in the GitHub repository (*https://github.com/microservices-aspnetcore/locationservice*) for the location service. I cannot stress enough how important it is that you and your team be able to automatically run all of your unit and integration tests in a reliable, reproducible environment. This is *key* to rapid iteration when building microservices for the cloud.

Exercising the Data Service

Running the data service should be relatively easy. The first thing we're going to need to do is spin up a running instance of Postgres. If you were paying attention to the *wercker.yml* file for the location service that sets up the integration tests, then you might be able to guess at the docker run command to start Postgres with our preferred parameters:

```
$ docker run -p 5432:5432 --name some-postgres \
  -e POSTGRES_PASSWORD=inteword -e POSTGRES_USER=integrator \
  -e POSTGRES_DB=locationservice -d postgres
```

This starts the Postgres Docker image with the name some-postgres (this will be important shortly). To verify that we can connect to Postgres, we can run the following Docker command to launch psql:

```
$ docker run -it --rm --link some-postgres:postgres postgres \
  psql -h postgres -U integrator -d locationservice
Password for user integrator:
psql (9.6.2)
Type "help" for help.

locationservice=# select 1;
 ?column?
----------
        1
(1 row)
```

With the database up and running, we need a schema. The tables in which we expect to store the migration metadata and our location records don't yet exist. To put them in the database, we just need to run an EF Core command from the location service's project directory. Note that we're also setting environment variables that we'll need soon:

```
$ export TRANSIENT=false
$ export POSTGRES__CSTR="Host=localhost;Username=integrator; \
  Password=inteword;Database=locationservice;Port=5432"
$ dotnet ef database update

Build succeeded.
```

```
    0 Warning(s)
    0 Error(s)

Time Elapsed 00:00:03.25
info: Startup[0]
      Using 'Host=localhost;Username=integrator;
Password=inteword;Port=5432;Database=locationservice' for DB
 connection string.
Executed DbCommand (13ms) [Parameters=[], CommandType='Text',
 CommandTimeout='30']
SELECT EXISTS (SELECT 1 FROM pg_catalog.pg_class c
JOIN pg_catalog.pg_namespace n ON n.oid=c.relnamespace WHERE
 c.relname='__EFMigrationsHistory');
Executed DbCommand (56ms) [Parameters=[], CommandType='Text',
 CommandTimeout='30']
CREATE TABLE "__EFMigrationsHistory" (
    "MigrationId" varchar(150) NOT NULL,
    "ProductVersion" varchar(32) NOT NULL,
    CONSTRAINT "PK___EFMigrationsHistory" PRIMARY KEY
("MigrationId")
);
Executed DbCommand (0ms) [Parameters=[], CommandType='Text',
CommandTimeout='30']
SELECT EXISTS (SELECT 1 FROM pg_catalog.pg_class c JOIN
 pg_catalog.pg_namespace n ON n.oid=c.relnamespace WHERE
 c.relname='__EFMigrationsHistory');
Executed DbCommand (2ms) [Parameters=[], CommandType='Text',
CommandTimeout='30']
SELECT "MigrationId", "ProductVersion"
FROM "__EFMigrationsHistory"
ORDER BY "MigrationId";
Applying migration '20160917140258_Initial'.
Executed DbCommand (19ms) [Parameters=[], CommandType='Text',
CommandTimeout='30']
CREATE EXTENSION IF NOT EXISTS "uuid-ossp";
Executed DbCommand (18ms) [Parameters=[], CommandType='Text',
CommandTimeout='30']
CREATE TABLE "LocationRecords" (
    "ID" uuid NOT NULL,
    "Altitude" float4 NOT NULL,
    "Latitude" float4 NOT NULL,
    "Longitude" float4 NOT NULL,
    "MemberID" uuid NOT NULL,
    "Timestamp" int8 NOT NULL,
    CONSTRAINT "PK_LocationRecords" PRIMARY KEY ("ID")
);
Executed DbCommand (0ms) [Parameters=[], CommandType='Text',
 CommandTimeout='30']
INSERT INTO "__EFMigrationsHistory" ("MigrationId",
"ProductVersion")
VALUES ('20160917140258_Initial', '1.1.1');
Done.
```

At this point Postgres is running with a valid schema and it's ready to start accepting commands from the location service. Here's where it gets a *little* tricky. If we're going to run the location service from inside a Docker image, then referring to the Postgres server's host as localhost won't work—because that's the host *inside* the Docker image.

What we need is for the location service to reach *out* of its container and then *into* the Postgres container. We can do this with a container link that creates a virtual hostname (we'll call it postgres), but we'll need to change our environment variable before launching the Docker image:

```
$ export POSTGRES__CSTR="Host=postgres;Username=integrator; \
Password=inteword;Database=locationservice;Port=5432"
$ docker run -p 5000:5000 --link some-postgres:postgres \
  -e TRANSIENT=false -e PORT=5000 \
  -e POSTGRES__CSTR dotnetcoreservices/locationservice:latest
```

Now that we've linked the service's container to the Postgres container via the post gres hostname, the location service should have no trouble connecting to the database.

To see this all in action, let's submit a location record (as usual, take the line feeds out of this command when you type it):

```
$ curl -H "Content-Type:application/json" -X POST -d \
  '{"id":"64c3e69f-1580-4b2f-a9ff-2c5f3b8f0e1f","latitude":12.0, \
    "longitude":10.0,"altitude":5.0,"timestamp":0, \
    "memberId":"63e7acf8-8fae-42ce-9349-3c8593ac8292"}' \
  http://localhost:5000/locations/63e7acf8-8fae-42ce-9349-3c8593ac8292

{"id":"64c3e69f-1580-4b2f-a9ff-2c5f3b8f0e1f",
 "latitude":12.0,"longitude":10.0,"altitude":5.0,
 "timestamp":0,"memberID":"63e7acf8-8fae-42ce-9349-3c8593ac8292"}
```

Take a look at the trace output from your running Docker image for the location service. You should see some very useful Entity Framework trace data explaining what happened. The service performed a SQL INSERT, so things are looking promising:

```
info: Microsoft.EntityFrameworkCore.Storage.
IRelationalCommandBuilderFactory[1]
      Executed DbCommand (23ms)
[Parameters=[@p0='?', @p1='?', @p2='?', @p3='?', @p4='?', @p5='?'],
 CommandType='Text', CommandTimeout='30']
      INSERT INTO "LocationRecords" ("ID", "Altitude", "Latitude",
"Longitude", "MemberID", "Timestamp")
      VALUES (@p0, @p1, @p2, @p3, @p4, @p5);
info: Microsoft.AspNetCore.Mvc.Internal.ObjectResultExecutor[1]
      Executing ObjectResult, writing value Microsoft.AspNetCore
.Mvc.ControllerContext.
info: Microsoft.AspNetCore.Mvc.Internal.ControllerActionInvoker[2]
      Executed action StatlerWaldorfCorp.LocationService.
```

```
Controllers.LocationRecordController.AddLocation
(StatlerWaldorfCorp.LocationService) in 2253.7616ms
info: Microsoft.AspNetCore.Hosting.Internal.WebHost[2]
      Request finished in 2602.7855ms 201 application/json;
charset=utf-8
```

Let's ask the service for this fictitious member's location history:

```
$ curl http://localhost:5000/locations/63e7acf8-8fae-42ce-9349-3c8593ac8292
```

```
[{"id":"64c3e69f-1580-4b2f-a9ff-2c5f3b8f0e1f",
  "latitude":12.0,"longitude":10.0,"altitude":5.0,
  "timestamp":0,"memberID":"63e7acf8-8fae-42ce-9349-3c8593ac8292"}]
```

The corresponding Entity Framework trace looks like this:

```
info: Microsoft.EntityFrameworkCore.Storage.
IRelationalCommandBuilderFactory[1]
      Executed DbCommand (23ms) [Parameters=[@__memberId_0='?'],
  CommandType='Text', CommandTimeout='30']
      SELECT "lr"."ID", "lr"."Altitude", "lr"."Latitude",
  "lr"."Longitude", "lr"."MemberID", "lr"."Timestamp"
      FROM "LocationRecords" AS "lr"
      WHERE "lr"."MemberID" = @__memberId_0
      ORDER BY "lr"."Timestamp"
```

Just to be double sure, let's query the latest endpoint to make sure we still get what we expect to see:

```
$ curl http://localhost:5000/locations/63e7acf8-8fae-42ce-9349-3c8593ac8292 \
/latest
```

```
{"id":"64c3e69f-1580-4b2f-a9ff-2c5f3b8f0e1f",
  "latitude":12.0,"longitude":10.0,"altitude":5.0,
  "timestamp":0,"memberID":"63e7acf8-8fae-42ce-9349-3c8593ac8292"}
```

Finally, to prove that we really are using real database persistence and that this isn't just a random fluke, use docker ps and docker kill to locate the Docker process for the location service and kill it. Restart it using the exact same command you used before.

You should now be able to query the location service and get the exact same data you had before. Of course, once you stop the Postgres container you'll permanently lose that data.

Summary

There are no hard and fast rules about microservices that say we must communicate with a database, but exposure to the real world tells us that a lot of our microservices are going to sit on top of databases.

In this chapter we talked about some of the architectural and technical concerns with building a .NET Core microservice that exposes a RESTful API that interacts with a database. We illustrated how to use dependency injection to configure our repository service, as well as how to use build automation tools to run integration tests against clean, private database instances.

In the coming chapters, we'll start exploring more advanced topics as we widen the scope of our coverage of microservices from individual services to entire service ecosystems.

CHAPTER 6

Event Sourcing and CQRS

Technology can solve a lot of problems, but code, libraries, and languages alone are not enough to solve all of our problems. In this chapter, we're going to take a look at some design patterns that will prepare us for the kind of massive scale that cloud platforms facilitate.

We'll explore the motivations behind and philosophies of Event Sourcing (ES) and Command Query Responsibility Segregation (CQRS), and then we'll walk through some sample code that illustrates these design principles in action.

Introducing Event Sourcing

When we build software for a small scale, we tend to make a lot of assumptions. And when building microservices in a vacuum, especially if we're following some classic "hello world"–style samples, we often do things in a way that might not be conducive to scale.

For example, our location service is synchronous. We submit a new location to it and it immediately writes that location to a database. When we want to know location history or the most recent location, we query the same service and it in turn queries the database. On the surface nothing seems all that bad about this design, until we ask ourselves how this might hold up against a million new location records per day for thousands or tens of thousands of team members. At this scale, these queries and new location submissions are going to be agonizingly slow, and we'll quickly get bogged down waiting for the database.

This type of situation is what we call *monolithic thinking*. Even though we're using microservices in the technical sense, we're definitely not taking full advantage of the cloud, or of truly robust distributed computing design patterns. In short, we're just making *smaller monoliths*, or, as some might call them, *microliths*.[1]

To help explain how Event Sourcing works, we'll use an analogy: reality itself.

Reality Is Event Sourced

Our brains are essentially event-sourced systems. We receive stimuli in the form of the five senses, and our brains are then responsible for properly sequencing each stimulus (an *event*). Every few hundred milliseconds or so, they perform some calculations against this never-ending stream of stimuli. The result of these calculations is what we call *reality*.

Our minds process the incoming *event stream* and then compute *state*. This state is what we perceive as our reality; the world around us. When we watch someone dancing to music, we're receiving audio and visual events, ensuring they're in the proper order (our minds compensate for the fact that we process audio and visual stimuli at different speeds, giving us the illusion of synchronized stimuli).

Event-sourced applications operate in a similar manner. They consume streams of incoming events, perform functions against the inbound streams, and compute results or state in response. This is a very different model than microliths that just expose simple, synchronous query and store–type operations.

Event Sourcing Defined

There are a number of extremely good sources of information available on Event Sourcing. ES is not a brand new pattern. It is, however, gaining new traction as a viable way to deal with the types of elastic scaling and reliability that are required by cloud services.

The goal of this chapter isn't to provide you with an in-depth doctoral thesis on the topic, but to give you enough of an overview so that the code we're going to write will make sense, both from a technical and an architectural viewpoint.

In what we think of as traditional applications, state is managed as a discrete set of data. If a client makes a PUT or POST request to our service, the state is mutated. This gives us a good sense of how things are *right now*, but doesn't give us any indication of how we got there. Also, remember that the concept of *right now* is an illusion, so attempting to bend reality to support this notion may be counterproductive.

Event Sourcing takes care of that problem, and much more, by separating the concern of state management from the concern of receiving stimuli that result in state

---

1 These are services that are micro in nature but don't embrace the Single Responsibility Principle.

changes. To make this happen, there are a number of requirements for an event-sourced system. It must be outlined in the following list:

Ordered

> Event streams are ordered. Performing calculations against the same set of events but in a different sequence will produce different output. For this reason, ordering and proper time management are essential.

Idempotent

> Any function that operates on an event stream *must* always return the exact same result for identical ordered event streams. This rule is absolutely mandatory, and failing to abide by it will cause untold levels of disaster.

Isolated

> Any function that produces a result based on an event stream *cannot* make use of external information. All data required for calculations *must* be present in the events.

Past tense

> Events take place in the past. This should be reflected in your variable names, structure names, and architecture. Event processors run calculations against a chronologically ordered sequence of events *that have already happened.*

Put mathematically, a function that operates on a stream of events will always produce the same state and output set of new events. For example:

```
f(event¹, event², ...) = state¹ + { output event set }
```

In keeping with the rules of Event Sourcing, this function, given the same inputs, will always produce the same outputs. This makes the business logic core of any Event Sourcing system eminently testable and reliable, whereas in most legacy codebases the business logic layer of the application is the least tested, darkest and scariest place.

As a corollary to this, you can add that given an existing state and an inbound event stream, an event processing function will always produce the same predictable state and set of output events:

```
f(state¹, event¹, event², ...) = state² + { output event set }
```

A few concrete examples might help further illustrate how the world looks when you see problems as event sourced. Let's take a financial transaction processing system as a sample. We could have an inbound stream of transactions, the processing of which results in state changes such as modifications of account balances, credit limits, and so on. Such a transaction processing system might also emit new events to different streams as a result of processing, allowing partner systems to be notified and possibly triggering push notifications to customers with banking applications on their mobile devices.

The popular blockchain (e.g., Bitcoin) technology is based on the idea of *secure* and *trusted* sequences of events that occur on some owned resource.

Let's take another of our most favorite problem domains: the Internet of Things (IoT). For the sake of illustration we can assume that we have an incoming stream of events from our smart devices containing data like GPS coordinates, weather statistics, and other sensor measurements. This event processor has two functions. First, it takes the latest recorded measurements, makes them available for a cache (this applies to CQRS, which we'll get to shortly), and monitors the data in the stream for alert conditions. Then, when these conditions occur, it emits events so that other parts of the system can react accordingly.

Learning to Love Eventual Consistency

Shifting the paradigm to viewing the world as a series of streams upon which you place event processors and even more event emitters can be a shock to even the most seasoned developers.

In an event-sourced system, you don't get to perform simple CRUD (Create, Read, Update, Delete) operations in a synchronous fashion against one or more services. There is no immediate feedback from the system of record that gives you the concrete state of how things exist in a consistent manner.

Instead, things in this new world are *eventually consistent*. You probably experience eventually consistent systems on a daily basis and never give them much thought because they are so commonplace.

Your banking system is eventually consistent: *eventually* the transaction where you just purchased that shiny new computer will show up in your bank account, *eventually* causing you pain... but until then you can enjoy that new laptop smell with no remorse.

Other eventually consistent applications with which we all interact daily are social networking apps. You've probably seen the scenario where a comment or post you make from one device takes a few minutes to show up in a friend's browser or device. This is because the application architects have decided on a trade-off: by giving up the immediate consistency of synchronous operation in favor of a tolerable delay in feedback, the application is able to support enormous scale and traffic volume.

Learning to embrace and trust eventual consistency involves a thorough analysis of what information your users need and, more importantly, *when* they need it. It is up to you and your deep knowledge of your problem domain to decide on what information needs to be available immediately and which information can lag.

This leads us to our next pattern: CQRS.

The CQRS Pattern

If we follow some of the patterns we've been talking about to a logical conclusion, we will arrive at the need for the separation of command inputs from queries in our system, otherwise known as the *Command Query Responsibility Segregation* pattern.

The idea is a simple one, but like Event Sourcing, it often results in a fundamental shift in how we think about distributed systems. Commands are responsible for submitting inputs into our system, which will likely result in the creation of events distributed to one or more streams.

We've already decided that we're going to sacrifice immediate consistency for scale, so we know that the act of submitting a command should be a fire-and-forget operation. The response from submitting a command is not the newly altered (consistent) state, it is merely an acknowledgment of whether or not the command was successfully ingested by the system.

Eventually, the state of the system will be altered to reflect the processing of this one command. The size of this time lapse depends entirely on the business process being performed and the criticality of the propagation of the data change.

The other half of this new segmentation of responsibilities is the *query*. As a result of embracing eventual consistency, we've already done an in-depth analysis of the information our clients need.

Acknowledging the Imperfection of Design

While we might have performed an in-depth analysis of the information our customers need, when they need it, and why, this knowledge will *never* be perfect. We need to gather enough knowledge to *get started* building systems.

Once started, we can deploy, gather feedback, and iterate rapidly to improve the system. If we wait to start building until we have the mythical "perfect knowledge" of the final state of our system, we will be doomed to repeat the mistakes of the past and crippled by analysis paralysis.

Since we know what queries are going to be made of our system, we can predict those queries and, in many cases, make the data available *before* the client queries for it.

This is another fundamental shift in thinking. Traditional backend monolithic applications involve hitting a query endpoint with some parameters. Those parameters are then used to perform some amount of lengthy processing and querying, returning calculated results.

In the world of massive scale, volume, and throughput we simply can't afford to tie up the resources of our microservices by making computationally expensive queries. We're no longer going to tolerate sitting around twiddling our thumbs while we wait for our filter and grouping clauses to sift through millions of rows of data that might be incurring row- or table-level locks in a database.

The idea is to front-run the expected usage of the system so that the data is made available *as close to the consumer* as possible, and in a way that is queryable as fast as possible, involving the smallest amount of computational processing as possible. In short, we want the queries to be *as dumb as possible*.

Let's use another example to illustrate this pattern in action. Imagine that we're writing some facilities management software for apartment buildings. Tenants will be accessing a portal that allows for a display of electrical usage. Depending on who logs in, we'll be able to see monthly usage values by apartment, by building, by region, etc.

We've got an event stream of events from electrical usage monitoring devices. Each unit might contribute one usage event every hour (since kWh is an accepted standard for metered electricity usage). We *could* build this system such that every time someone refreshes their portal page, we go out to some data service and request a roll-up of all the meter events within some time frame, but that is just unacceptable for modern software development at cloud scale.

If we're pushing these calculations off to a database, then our database immediately becomes a critical point of failure and will gum up our otherwise smooth machinery.

Knowing the usage pattern of the majority of our customers gives us the ability to take advantage of Event Sourcing and build a proper CQRS implementation. Our event processor can recompute cached meter aggregates every time it receives a new event. With this in place, we'll have the results portal users are expecting *already sitting in a database or cache* when the query happens. No complex calculations, no ad hoc aggregates and complicated roll-ups... just a simple query.

The event store (persistent storage of all meter events received since the system started) is still available if we need more complex calculations or auditing, but the eventually consistent state (aka *reality*) is made available for immediate, super-fast query to all consumers.

Event Sourcing and CQRS in Action—Team Proximity Sample

Up to this point in the book all of our samples have been fairly simple. We've dealt with simple services that perform simple tasks. They are small and we can deploy them to the cloud, and we can even scale them up and down so we can handle larger volumes.

But this type of architecture only gets us so far. For the rest of this chapter we're going to expand the scope of our team management application so that we can illustrate the power (and potential downfalls) of Event Sourcing and CQRS applied to a real-world problem.

The problem with applying buzzword-ridden patterns to our problems is that the application of these patterns is often done at too high a level. Most of us have fallen into the trap of doing some reading, finding a fancy new pattern, and then slathering it on top of an existing solution without doing much analysis. This is the classic "I have a hammer and everything looks like nails" fallacy.

In these situations, we tend to apply shiny new patterns like condiments. We sprinkle them on top of our legacy applications and hope they will run better, respond faster, and scale more. The problem is patterns like the ones we're discussing in this book aren't toppings you shake onto existing code; they require a fundamental change in the recipe. For many organizations that have built up years of process around the creation of hard-to-scale monoliths, implementing them might also require building completely new kitchens.

Event Sourcing Is Not a Panacea

While we're devoting a lot of time to discussing ES, CQRS, and eventual consistency, these are patterns that need to be applied when the problem domain requires it. These patterns, like all patterns, are just some possible solutions to a problem. Assuming that you can fix all problems with Event Sourcing is as dangerous as assuming you can solve all real-world problems with a single hammer.

The samples for our existing team and location services are rudimentary. They let us update and query team membership as well as member locations. But let's say our application now needs to manage a vast number of teams, each containing hundreds of individuals. Each member of a team is wielding a mobile device with an application that routinely reports the location of that member.

While having near-real-time location data on all of the people using our application is a great feature on its own, the real power comes from what we can do by processing incoming events. In our case, we want to detect when two team members are close to each other.

In the new sample we're going to build, we will be detecting when member locations occur within some small distance of each other. The system will then support reacting to these proximity detections. For example, we might want to send push notifications to the mobile devices of the nearby team members to alert them to the possibility for catching up in person.

To do this properly, we're going to embrace Event Sourcing and CQRS, and we'll be splitting up the responsibilities of the system among four components, as follows:

- The location reporter service (Command)
- The event processor (Event Sourcing)
- The reality service (Query)
- The proximity monitor (Event Sourcing)

We will discuss the purpose and implementation of each of these services in detail throughout the rest of the chapter.

The Location Reporter Service

In a CQRS system, the inputs and outputs of the system are decoupled entirely. For our sample, the inputs take the form of *commands* sent to the location reporter service.

The client applications (mobile, web, IoT, etc.) in our system need to submit new location data on members on a regular basis. They will do so by sending updates to the location reporter.

You can find the full source code for the location reporter on GitHub (*https://github.com/microservices-aspnetcore/es-locationreporter*).

Since we build everything API First, let's take a look at the extremely simple API for the location reporter, shown in Table 6-1.

Table 6-1. Location reporter service API

Resource	Method	Description
/api/members/{memberId}/locationreports	POST	Submits a new location report

When we get a new location report, we'll perform the following tasks:

1. Validate the report object.
2. Convert the command into an event.
3. Emit the event on a message queue.

Recall from the discussion about the requirements of an event sourcing system that event processing cannot make use of information that exists outside the event stream.

This sample is designed to detect nearby teammates. This should bring up an important question: how do we know the team membership of the member referenced by a location report?

We could include it in the location report, but that would burden the client with maintaining information that isn't really part of the client's responsibility or domain.

Let's say we have a simple IoT device designed to emit GPS coordinates every 30 seconds. Should this physical device then also be required to periodically query a service to discover team membership?

You'll often hear this problem referred to as a *complexity leak*. The internal workings (or limitations) of our system could leak out of our service and force our clients to bear the burden of additional complexity. There is also an important Conway's law (*https://en.wikipedia.org/wiki/Conway%27s_law*) potential for failure here. If the team responsible for the service and the consuming client are isolated, then it becomes almost too easy for the service team to foist the complexity on the client and not give the problem the thought and diligence it requires.

So, if the event processor (we'll discuss that next) can't query for team membership while processing the event stream because of the core rules of Event Sourcing, and the client/consumers shouldn't bear the burden of maintaining team membership, what do we do?

As you work with reactive, distributed systems more and more, you will see this pattern emerge consistently. Solving this particular problem—gathering all the necessary information to produce an event—should be the responsibility of the command processor, the thing that turns commands into events.

In our case, the command processor needs to create an event with an appropriate timestamp, and it's also going to need to fetch the team membership (which is a volatile quantity, subject to change at any time) to place that information on the event.

This has the desirable effect of allowing our system to detect nearby team members *only if they were on the same team at the time the events occurred*. Other solutions to this problem that might not utilize Event Sourcing could produce "false positive" proximity alerts for team members based on stale caches, out-of-order message processing, client synchronization issues, etc.

While the consequences of a false positive for a harmless alert about a nearby teammate might be low, think about if this application served a different business domain. What if this was a financial application processing an event stream of transactions, or a security system granting or denying physical access? In these cases, the consequences of a false positive based on out-of-stream data could be disastrous.

Creating the location reports controller

Now that we know what we're building and why, let's take a look at the simple controller that handles our single-method API (Example 6-1).

Example 6-1. LocationReportsController.cs

```csharp
using System;
using Microsoft.AspNetCore.Mvc;
using StatlerWaldorfCorp.LocationReporter.Events;
using StatlerWaldorfCorp.LocationReporter.Models;
using StatlerWaldorfCorp.LocationReporter.Services;

namespace StatlerWaldorfCorp.LocationReporter.Controllers
{
[Route("/api/members/{memberId}/locationreports")]
public class LocationReportsController : Controller
{
    private ICommandEventConverter converter;
    private IEventEmitter eventEmitter;
    private ITeamServiceClient teamServiceClient;


    public LocationReportsController(
        ICommandEventConverter converter,
        IEventEmitter eventEmitter,
        ITeamServiceClient teamServiceClient) {

        this.converter = converter;
        this.eventEmitter = eventEmitter;
        this.teamServiceClient = teamServiceClient;
    }

    [HttpPost]
    public ActionResult PostLocationReport(Guid memberId,
      [FromBody]LocationReport locationReport)
    {
      MemberLocationRecordedEvent locationRecordedEvent =
        converter.CommandToEvent(locationReport);
      locationRecordedEvent.TeamID =
        teamServiceClient.GetTeamForMember(
            locationReport.MemberID);
      eventEmitter.EmitLocationRecordedEvent(
        locationRecordedEvent);

      return this.Created(
        $"/api/members/{memberId}/locationreports/
        {locationReport.ReportID}",
        locationReport);
    }
}
}
```

The controller is really just responsible for handling the incoming JSON payload, delegating the work, and replying with an appropriate JSON response. As you can see in the code, we've made a couple of utilities available for injection at runtime and during testing, like the `ICommandEventConverter`, the `IEventEmitter`, and the `ITeamService Client`.

While this pattern may not have been commonplace in the past with legacy ASP.NET applications, you will see this all over modern ASP.NET (especially ASP.NET Core) code. We inject the objects to which we will delegate and we leave our controller methods as simple and small as possible. This makes our controllers and our utilities far easier to test and maintain.

The command converter creates a basic event from an input command while the team service client allows us to fetch the ID of the team to which the member belongs (our system only allows people to belong to one team at a time). Finally, the event emitter is responsible for sending the event to the right place.

Because all of these things are injectable via DI and available for constructor injection during unit tests, we can very easily make our code simple, readable, and easy to maintain.

Building an AMQP event emitter

The location reporter service is actually pretty small, and other than the controller, the most interesting stuff is in the event emitter. Our sample emits events to an Advanced Message Queuing Protocol (AMQP) queue supported by RabbitMQ. Take a look at the code for our AMQP event emitter (Example 6-2).

Example 6-2. AMQPEventEmitter.cs

```
using System;
using System.Linq;
using System.Text;
using Microsoft.Extensions.Logging;
using Microsoft.Extensions.Options;
using RabbitMQ.Client;
using StatlerWaldorfCorp.LocationReporter.Models;

namespace StatlerWaldorfCorp.LocationReporter.Events
{
    public class AMQPEventEmitter : IEventEmitter
    {
        private readonly ILogger logger;
        private AMQPOptions rabbitOptions;
        private ConnectionFactory connectionFactory;

        public AMQPEventEmitter(ILogger<AMQPEventEmitter> logger,
            IOptions<AMQPOptions> amqpOptions)
        {
            this.logger = logger;
            this.rabbitOptions = amqpOptions.Value;
```

```
    connectionFactory = new ConnectionFactory();

    connectionFactory.UserName = rabbitOptions.Username;
    connectionFactory.Password = rabbitOptions.Password;
    connectionFactory.VirtualHost =
      rabbitOptions.VirtualHost;
    connectionFactory.HostName = rabbitOptions.HostName;
    connectionFactory.Uri = rabbitOptions.Uri;

    logger.LogInformation(
      "AMQP Event Emitter configured with URI {0}",
      rabbitOptions.Uri);
  }
public const string QUEUE_LOCATIONRECORDED =
  "memberlocationrecorded";

public void EmitLocationRecordedEvent(
  MemberLocationRecordedEvent locationRecordedEvent)
{
    using (IConnection conn = connectionFactory.
      CreateConnection()) {
        using (IModel channel = conn.CreateModel()) {
            channel.QueueDeclare(
                queue: QUEUE_LOCATIONRECORDED,
                durable: false,
                exclusive: false,
                autoDelete: false,
                arguments: null
            );
            string jsonPayload =
              locationRecordedEvent.toJson();
            var body =
              Encoding.UTF8.GetBytes(jsonPayload);
            channel.BasicPublish(
                exchange: "",
                routingKey: QUEUE_LOCATIONRECORDED,
                basicProperties: null,
                body: body
            );
        }
    }
  }
}
}
}
```

As with our controller, we're injecting the supporting classes we need by interface as parameters to our constructor. None of this would work properly if we didn't configure dependency injection in our startup class.

Configuring and starting the service

The AMQP event emitter class gets the information needed to configure a RabbitMQ connection factory from an options instance. You can see how these options are configured by looking at the location reporter's Startup class (Example 6-3).

Example 6-3. src/StatlerWaldorfCorp.LocationReporter/Startup.cs

```
using Microsoft.AspNetCore.Builder;
using Microsoft.AspNetCore.Hosting;
using Microsoft.Extensions.Configuration;
using Microsoft.Extensions.DependencyInjection;
using System;
using Microsoft.Extensions.Logging;
using System.Linq;
using StatlerWaldorfCorp.LocationReporter.Models;
using StatlerWaldorfCorp.LocationReporter.Events;
using StatlerWaldorfCorp.LocationReporter.Services;

namespace StatlerWaldorfCorp.LocationReporter
{
    public class Startup
    {
        public Startup(IHostingEnvironment env,
          ILoggerFactory loggerFactory)
        {
            loggerFactory.AddConsole();
            loggerFactory.AddDebug();

            var builder = new ConfigurationBuilder()
                .SetBasePath(env.ContentRootPath)
                .AddJsonFile("appsettings.json",
                    optional: false, reloadOnChange: false)
                .AddEnvironmentVariables();

            Configuration = builder.Build();
        }

        public IConfigurationRoot Configuration { get; }

        public void ConfigureServices(IServiceCollection services)
        {
            services.AddMvc();
            services.AddOptions();

            services
              .Configure<AMQPOptions>(
                Configuration.GetSection("amqp"));
            services
              .Configure<TeamServiceOptions>(
                Configuration.GetSection("teamservice"));
```

```
            services.AddSingleton(typeof(IEventEmitter),
               typeof(AMQPEventEmitter));
            services.AddSingleton(typeof(ICommandEventConverter),
               typeof(CommandEventConverter));
            services.AddSingleton(typeof(ITeamServiceClient),
               typeof(HttpTeamServiceClient));
        }

        public void Configure(IApplicationBuilder app,
                IHostingEnvironment env,
                ILoggerFactory loggerFactory,
                ITeamServiceClient teamServiceClient,
                IEventEmitter eventEmitter)
        {
            // Asked for instances of singletons during startup
            // to force initialization early.

            app.UseMvc();
        }
    }
}
```

The most important lines of code are in bold. The first two calls to `Configure` tell the configuration subsystem that it should make options instances available for dependency injection based on the `amqp` and `teamservice` sections, respectively.

Remember that these sections can be supplied by an *appsettings.json* file but can also be overridden by environment variables. This environment variable overriding is what we would do in a production environment to point the app at the right Rabbit server and team service URL.

You may also notice that we're reading in an *appsettings.json* file. This file contains a *default* set of values to configure our RabbitMQ service as well as the URL to the team service for our queries. It's important to remember that the order of precedence is defined by the order in which you add configuration sources, so make sure that you always add your local/default JSON settings *first* so they can be overridden.

Here's what our *appsettings.json* file looks like:

```
{
  "amqp": {
    "username": "guest",
    "password": "guest",
    "hostname": "localhost",
    "uri": "amqp://localhost:5672/",
    "virtualhost": "/"
  },
  "teamservice": {
    "url": "http://localhost:5001"
  }
```

```
}
```

Consuming the team service

Before we get to running the location reporter, let's take a look at the HTTP implementation of the ITeamServiceClient (Example 6-4). Note that we're getting the
URL of the team service from injected configuration options, the same way we configured our Rabbit client.

Example 6-4. HttpTeamServiceClient.cs

```
using System;
using Microsoft.Extensions.Logging;
using Microsoft.Extensions.Options;
using System.Linq;
using System.Net.Http;
using System.Net.Http.Headers;
using Newtonsoft.Json;
using StatlerWaldorfCorp.LocationReporter.Models;

namespace StatlerWaldorfCorp.LocationReporter.Services
{
    public class HttpTeamServiceClient : ITeamServiceClient
    {
        private readonly ILogger logger;

        private HttpClient httpClient;

        public HttpTeamServiceClient(
            IOptions<TeamServiceOptions> serviceOptions,
            ILogger<HttpTeamServiceClient> logger)
        {
            this.logger = logger;

            var url = serviceOptions.Value.Url;

            logger.LogInformation(
              "Team Service HTTP client using URL {0}",
              url);

            httpClient = new HttpClient();
            httpClient.BaseAddress = new Uri(url);
        }
        public Guid GetTeamForMember(Guid memberId)
        {
            httpClient.DefaultRequestHeaders.Accept.Clear();
            httpClient.DefaultRequestHeaders.Accept.Add(
              new MediaTypeWithQualityHeaderValue(
                "application/json"));
```

```
            HttpResponseMessage response =
              httpClient.GetAsync(
              String.Format("/members/{0}/team",
                memberId)).Result;

            TeamIDResponse teamIdResponse;
            if (response.IsSuccessStatusCode) {
                string json = response.Content
                  .ReadAsStringAsync().Result;
                teamIdResponse =
                  JsonConvert.DeserializeObject<TeamIDResponse>(
                    json);
                return teamIdResponse.TeamID;
            }
            else {
                return Guid.Empty;
            }
        }
    }

    public class TeamIDResponse
    {
        public Guid TeamID { get; set; }
    }
}
```

In this example we're using the `.Result` property to force a thread to block while we wait for a reply from the asynchronous method. For production-quality code, we would probably refactor this and ensure that we're carrying asynchronous results all the way to the service boundary.

The code in bold shows the most important piece of this client: we're asking the team service to tell us the team membership of a member. This REST resource wasn't part of the service when we designed it earlier; it was added later to support the functionality for this chapter.

To see the location reporter in action, we first need to set up a local copy of RabbitMQ. We could also just go straight to writing integration tests and rely on the cloud-based Wercker builds to fire up the RabbitMQ testing instance, but I like being able to play with things locally first to get a feel for how everything works.

If you're on a Mac, it should be easy enough to either install RabbitMQ or just start up a Docker image running Rabbit with the management console plug-in enabled (make sure to map both the management console port and the regular port). On Windows, it's probably easiest to just install RabbitMQ locally. For details on how to install or run Rabbit, check out the documentation (*http://rabbitmq.com/*).

Running the location reporter service

With that running, and our defaults set up to point to a local Rabbit instance, we can fire up the location reporter service as follows (make sure you're in the *src/StatlerWaldorfCorp.LocationReporter* subdirectory):

```
$ dotnet restore
...
$ dotnet build
...
$ dotnet run --server.urls=http://0.0.0.0:9090
...
```

Depending on your setup, you might not need to change the default port. With the service running, we just need to submit a request to the service. One of the easiest ways to do that is to install the Postman plug-in for Chrome, or we can use `curl` to submit a JSON payload like this one:

```
$ curl -X POST -d \
  '{"reportID": "...", \
    "origin": "...", "latitude": 10, "longitude": 20, \
    "memberID": "..."}' \
  http://...1e2 \
  /locationreports
```

When we submit this, we should get an HTTP 201 reply from the service, with the `Location` header set to something that looks like `/api/members/4da420c6-fa0f-4754-9643-8302401821e2/locationreports/f74be394-0d03-4a2f-bb55-7ce680f31d7e`. If everything else is working properly, we should be able to use our RabbitMQ management console to see that there's a new message sitting in the `memberlocationrecorded` queue, as shown in Figure 6-1.

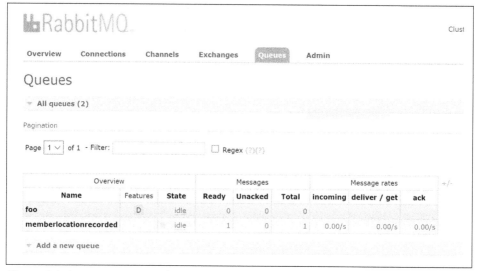

Figure 6-1. A new message in the queue

And if we use this same management console to examine the contents of the message, we should see that it is a faithful JSON conversion of the event we created, including the augmentations of the timestamp and the team membership of the member, as shown in Figure 6-2.

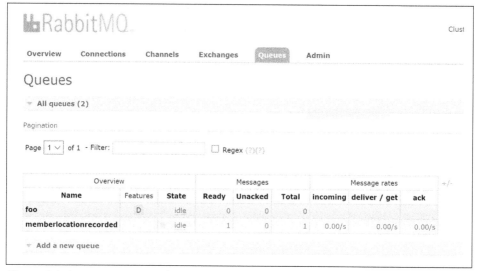

Figure 6-2. Getting a message from the queue

The Event Processor

The main purpose of the sample we're building in this chapter is to detect team members within some range of each other. The bulk of this work is done by the *event processor*. The event processor is the part of the system that is as close to a pure function as we can get.

It is responsible for consuming events from the stream and taking the appropriate actions. These actions could include emitting new events on new event streams or pushing state changes to the reality service (discussed next).

While there are many important pieces to the event processor, the core of it is the ability to detect nearby teammates. To perform that detection, we need to know how to compute the distance between their GPS coordinates.

Geolocation Calculations

We actually *don't* need to know how to compute the distance between GPS coordinates. Redis comes with a special type of list that stores GPS coordinates, and you can use commands like GEORADIUS and GEODIST to detect list members within a given radius and determine the distance between members.

In order to illustrate the role of an event processor, we're doing this calculation in the C# code, but in a production scenario we might defer this to Redis. Its geohashing calculations can detect nearby teammates *far* faster than we can do this in C#.

If you want to implement this for yourself as a fun experiment, you might want to try storing member locations in sets that correspond to their team membership; that way, querying GEORADIUS on a team's location set has the desired effect.

Rather than showing you the details of the math involved, Example 6-5 shows the unit test that proves the math we borrowed from the smart people on the internet works (if the Earth was flat, this math would be much easier!).

Example 6-5. GPS utility unit test

```
[Fact]
public void ProducesAccurateDistanceMeasurements()
{
  GpsUtility gpsUtility = new GpsUtility();

  GpsCoordinate losAngeles = new GpsCoordinate() {
      Latitude = 34.0522222,
      Longitude = -118.2427778
  };
```

```
GpsCoordinate newYorkCity = new GpsCoordinate() {
    Latitude = 40.7141667,
    Longitude = -74.0063889
};

double distance =
    gpsUtility.DistanceBetweenPoints(losAngeles, newYorkCity);
Assert.Equal(3933, Math.Round(distance)); // 3,933 km
Assert.Equal(0,
    gpsUtility.DistanceBetweenPoints(losAngeles, losAngeles));
}
```

In order to keep the code clean and testable, we want to separate the responsibilities of event processing into the following:

- Subscribing to a queue and obtaining new messages from the event stream
- Writing messages to the event store
- Processing the event stream (detecting proximity)
- Emitting messages to a queue as a result of stream processing
- Submitting state changes to the reality server/cache as a result of stream processing

As with all of this book's samples, you can find the full code for this on GitHub (*https://github.com/microservices-aspnetcore/es-proximitymonitor*). To save your eyes the agony of scanning through a dozen pages of code listings, I'll try and limit the listings to the most important pieces.

To detect proximity events, I've written a proximity detector that makes use of the GPS utility class (Example 6-6). It takes as input the event pulled from the stream, a list of teammates and their locations, and a radius threshold.

Example 6-6. ProximityDetector.cs

```
using System.Collections.Generic;
using StatlerWaldorfCorp.EventProcessor.Location;
using System.Linq;
using System;

namespace StatlerWaldorfCorp.EventProcessor.Events
{
    public class ProximityDetector
    {
        public ICollection<ProximityDetectedEvent>
            DetectProximityEvents(
                MemberLocationRecordedEvent memberLocationEvent,
                ICollection<MemberLocation> memberLocations,
                double distanceThreshold)
        {
```

```
GpsUtility gpsUtility = new GpsUtility();
GpsCoordinate sourceCoordinate = new GpsCoordinate() {
    Latitude = memberLocationEvent.Latitude,
    Longitude = memberLocationEvent.Longitude
};

return memberLocations.Where(
  ml => ml.MemberID != memberLocationEvent.MemberID &&
      gpsUtility.DistanceBetweenPoints(
          sourceCoordinate, ml.Location) <
          distanceThreshold)
  .Select( ml => {
    return new ProximityDetectedEvent() {
      SourceMemberID = memberLocationEvent.MemberID,
      TargetMemberID = ml.MemberID,
      DetectionTime = DateTime.UtcNow.Ticks,
      SourceMemberLocation = sourceCoordinate,
      TargetMemberLocation = ml.Location,
      MemberDistance =
        gpsUtility.DistanceBetweenPoints(
            sourceCoordinate, ml.Location)
      };
    }).ToList();
  }
 }
}
```

We can then take the results of this method and use them to create the appropriate side effects, including the optional dispatch of a `ProximityDetectedEvent` and the writing of an event to the event store.

In all of our code, we are embracing the principles behind clean object-oriented design and injecting dependencies into our classes by interface wherever possible. This makes the code readable, easier to maintain, and easier to test.

Case in point: the high-level code responsible for responding to an incoming message, detecting proximity events, and emitting proximity events and updating the reality cache is written so all of the real work is delegated to smaller classes that embody the Single Responsibility Principle.

Example 6-7 shows the code for our main event processor.

Example 6-7. Events/MemberLocationEventProcessor.cs

```csharp
using System;
using System.Collections.Generic;
using Microsoft.Extensions.Logging;
using StatlerWaldorfCorp.EventProcessor.Location;
using StatlerWaldorfCorp.EventProcessor.Queues;

namespace StatlerWaldorfCorp.EventProcessor.Events
{
public class MemberLocationEventProcessor : IEventProcessor
{
    private ILogger logger;
    private IEventSubscriber subscriber;
    private IEventEmitter eventEmitter;
    private ProximityDetector proximityDetector;
    private ILocationCache locationCache;

    public MemberLocationEventProcessor(
        ILogger<MemberLocationEventProcessor> logger,
        IEventSubscriber eventSubscriber,
        IEventEmitter eventEmitter,
        ILocationCache locationCache)
    {
        this.logger = logger;
        this.subscriber = eventSubscriber;
        this.eventEmitter = eventEmitter;
        this.proximityDetector = new ProximityDetector();
        this.locationCache = locationCache;

        this.subscriber.
          MemberLocationRecordedEventReceived += (mlre) => {
            var memberLocations =
                locationCache.GetMemberLocations(mlre.TeamID);
            ICollection<ProximityDetectedEvent> proximityEvents =
                proximityDetector.DetectProximityEvents(mlre,
                memberLocations, 30.0f);
            foreach (var proximityEvent in proximityEvents) {
                eventEmitter.
                  EmitProximityDetectedEvent(proximityEvent);
            }

            locationCache.Put(mlre.TeamID,
              new MemberLocation {
                MemberID = mlre.MemberID,
                Location = new GpsCoordinate {
                  Latitude = mlre.Latitude,
                  Longitude = mlre.Longitude
                }
            });
        };
```

```
    }

    public void Start()
    {
        this.subscriber.Subscribe();
    }

    public void Stop()
    {
        this.subscriber.Unsubscribe();
    }
}
}
```

The dependencies of this class are not only evident, but made mandatory through the use of the constructor parameters. They are:

- An instance of a logger appropriate for this class.
- An event subscriber (responsible for telling the processor when new `MemberLocationRecordedEvents` arrive).
- An event emitter, allowing the processor to emit `ProximityDetectedEvents`.
- A location cache, allowing us to quickly store and retrieve current locations of team members as discovered by the event processor. Depending on how you design your "reality" service, this cache can be shared by the reality service or a duplication of it.

The only other responsibility of the event processing service is that it should store every event it receives in the event store. There are a number of reasons for this, including providing a history for other services to search. The event store can also be used to reseed the reality cache if the cache crashes and loses data.

If you're feeling adventurous, you can look at the code created so far and follow the patterns used to add an event store interface to the `MemberLocationEventProcessor` class, making sure it's unit tested and the integration test verifies that events are being recorded.

Caches Are Only Conveniences

Remember that caches serve the architectural role of a convenience, and you should never have any data in a cache that you can't reconstitute from somewhere else. If your code encounters a cache miss, it should know how to go calculate what *should have been in the cache* and update the cache.

If your code won't work unless it gets a cache hit, then you might need to reevaluate your architecture or choose a different tool, like a full database for long-term persistence.

Since we've already covered how to build Entity Framework repositories in the book, I'll leave that code listing for you to check out on GitHub if you're curious.

The Redis location cache

The location cache interface has the following methods defined on it:

- GetMemberLocations(Guid teamId)
- Put(Guid teamId, MemberLocation location)

For our implementation of this cache I decided upon Redis, for a number of reasons. First and foremost, it's a very easy to use distributed cache. It's also incredibly powerful, and has very wide adoption and a thriving open source community around it. Finally, it is usually available in some form as a cloud-hosted solution, making it ideal for a backing service for our reality cache.

Redis is also quite a bit more than *just a cache*, and it includes a number of features that could dramatically improve the samples for this chapter that are out of scope of this book and better left to a book on Redis.

We're creating a Redis *hash* for each of the teams in our service. The JSON payload for a serialized member location is then added as a field (keyed on member ID) to this hash. This makes it easy to update multiple member locations simultaneously without creating a data-overwrite situation and makes it easy to query the list of locations for any given team, since the team is a hash.

Take a look at the following redis-cli session that was taken just moments after running some integration tests against a local instance on one of my development workstations:

```
127.0.0.1:6379> KEYS *
 1) "0145c13c-0dde-446c-ae8b-405a5fc33c76"
 2) "d23d529f-0c1e-470f-a316-403b934b98e9"
 3) "58265141-1859-41ef-8dfc-70b1e65e7d83"
 4) "26908092-cf9a-4c4f-b667-5086874c6b61"
 5) "679c3fdb-e673-4e9d-96dd-9a8388c76cc5"
 6) "f5cb73c5-f87c-4b97-b4e6-5319dc4db491"
 7) "56195441-168d-4b19-a110-1984f729596e"
 8) "49284102-36fd-49e6-a5fa-f622ee3708f1"
 9) "a4f4253b-df79-4f79-9eff-5d34a759f914"
10) "d13a6760-8043-408d-9a05-dd220988a655"
127.0.0.1:6379> HGETALL 0145c13c-0dde-446c-ae8b-405a5fc33c76
1) "7284050e-f320-40a5-b739-6a1ab4045768"
2) "{\"MemberID\":\"7284050e-f320-40a5-b739-6a1ab4045768\",
   \"Location\":{\"Latitude\":40.7141667,\"Longitude\":-74.0063889}}"
3) "2cde3be8-113f-4088-b2ba-5c5fc3ebada8"
4) "{\"MemberID\":\"2cde3be8-113f-4088-b2ba-5c5fc3ebada8\",
   \"Location\":{\"Latitude\":40.7282,\"Longitude\":-73.7949}}"
```

There are 10 hash keys displayed. Each of these hash keys is a team that has received at least one member location recorded event. Using the `HGETALL` command, we can get a list of all of the member location objects for that team.

For the full source code of the integration test that produced this data, take a look at the GitHub repository (*https://github.com/microservices-aspnetcore/es-eventprocessor*)

The Reality Service

Reality is subjective, and, as we discussed earlier, even reality as you perceive it in your mind is an approximation and actually occurs slightly in the past. In an effort to name our components in a way that respects this truth and the concept of eventual consistency, we've decided to call this service the *reality* service.

If we called it a state service or something else that implied that you could query it at any time and get a live, real-time, exact set of information that describes the state of the entire system at that moment, we would be misleading our consumers and the developers.

The reality service is responsible for maintaining the location of each team member, but that location will only be the most recently received location from some application. We will never know exactly where someone is; we can only tell where they were when they last submitted a command that produced a successfully processed event.

Again, this reinforces the notion that reality is really a function of stimuli received in the past.

Let's take a look at the API we want to expose from the reality service (Table 6-2).

Table 6-2. Reality service API

Resource	Method	Description
/api/reality/members	GET	Retrieves the last known location of all members that are known to the reality service
/api/reality/members/ {memberId}	GET	Retrieves the last known location of a single member
/api/reality/members/ {memberId}	PUT	Sets the last known location of a member

There are two important things to remember about a reality service like this:

Reality is not the event store.
> Reality is merely a representation of the state you expect your consumers to need, a prebuilt set of data designed to support the query operations in a CQRS pattern.

Reality is disposable.
> The reality cache that supports the query operations of the system is disposable. We should be able to destroy all instances of reality and reconstitute them simply by running our event processing algorithm against either an entire event stream, or the events occurring since the last snapshot.

The code for the reality service is made up of things we've covered already in this book:

- Basic microservice scaffolding (middleware, routing, configuration, bootstrapped web server)
- Reliance upon dependency injection to provide configuration options and implementation instances
- A class that talks to the Redis cache to query the current locations
- A consumer of the team service to query the list of teams

I'm not going to cover the specific code for the reality service because, as I said, everything in it is something that has been done elsewhere in the book. If you would like to build your own reality service as a reader exercise, I strongly encourage you to do so as this will help build your muscle memory for building out services from scratch in ASP.NET Core.

The Proximity Monitor

The output of the event processor is a stream of proximity detected events. In a real-world, production system, we would have some kind of application or service sitting on the end of this stream.

It would await the arrival of these events and then notify appropriate downstream components that the events have occurred. This could be a notification to a website to let a single-page app update its UI, or it could be a notification that gets sent to the mobile devices of both the source and target team members that are part of the event.

The code for a proximity monitor would include:

- Basic microservice scaffolding (this should be old hat to you by now)
- A queue consumer subscribed to the arrival of `ProximityDetectedEvent` messages
- Consumption of some third-party or cloud provider to deal with push notifications

Chapter 11 covers *real-time applications*, where we'll talk about some options for publishing and reacting to push notifications and integrating client-side applications with server applications in real time. We don't need to go into the code for a real proximity monitor for this chapter.

Running the Samples

There are a number of ways you can run the sample services created in this chapter to exercise everything you've learned so far. The easiest is to set it all up on your development workstation using locally installed services.

The following are the prerequisites for running the samples in this chapter:

A RabbitMQ server
> You can install this locally on your machine, you can run a copy of the Docker image available on docker hub (ensuring you bind the right ports), or you can point to a cloud-hosted RabbitMQ server.

A Redis server
> As with Rabbit, you can install this locally, run the Docker image, or point to a cloud-hosted Redis server.

The *appsettings.json* files for the services are checked into GitHub such that the default operating mode is to assume the prerequisites are running locally either through direct install or through ports exposed and mapped from running Docker images.

Refer to the instructions on the appropriate websites for either installing the servers or running the docker hub images. You do not need to do any configuration or setup beyond the defaults—the services all create their own hashes and queues.

Starting the Services

Once you've got your prerequisites up and running, check out the code for the services `es-locationreporter` and `es-eventprocessor` from GitHub. You'll also need to grab a copy of `teamservice`. Make sure you grab the `master` branch since you just want an in-memory repository for testing (the `location` branch requires a Postgres database).

As per usual procedure, make sure you do a `dotnet restore` and a `dotnet build` on the main service application for each of them from inside their respective *src/ <project>* directories.

To start the team service, issue the following command in a terminal from the *src/ StatlerWaldorfCorp.TeamService* directory:

```
$ dotnet run --server.urls=http://0.0.0.0:5001
Hosting environment: Production
Content root path: (...)
Now listening on: http://0.0.0.0:5001
Application started. Press Ctrl+C to shut down.
```

To start the location reporter, issue the following command at your terminal from the *src/StatlerWaldorfCorp.LocationReporter* directory:

```
$ dotnet run --server.urls=http://0.0.0.0:5002
info: StatlerWaldorfCorp.LocationReporter.Services
.HttpTeamServiceClient[0]
      Team Service HTTP client using URL http://localhost:5001
info: StatlerWaldorfCorp.LocationReporter.Events.AMQPEventEmitter[0]
      AMQP Event Emitter configured with URI amqp://localhost:5672/
Hosting environment: Production
Content root path: (...)
Now listening on: http://0.0.0.0:5002
Application started. Press Ctrl+C to shut down.
```

Note that it defaults to looking for the team service on port 5001. Because we're going to be running both microservices and both are ASP.NET services (even though the event processor just listens on queues), we need to make sure they don't try and grab the same server port.

Now start the event processor (from the *src/StatlerWaldorfCorp.EventProcessor* directory):

```
$ dotnet run --server.urls=http://0.0.0.0:5003
info: StatlerWaldorfCorp.EventProcessor.Queues.AMQP
.AMQPConnectionFactory[0]
      AMQP Connection configured for URI : amqp://localhost:5672/
info: StatlerWaldorfCorp.EventProcessor.Queues.AMQP
.AMQPEventSubscriber[0]
      Initialized event subscriber for queue memberlocationrecorded
info: StatlerWaldorfCorp.EventProcessor.Queues.AMQP
.AMQPConnectionFactory[0]
      AMQP Connection configured for URI : amqp://localhost:5672/
info: StatlerWaldorfCorp.EventProcessor.Queues.AMQP
.AMQPEventEmitter[0]
      Emitting events on queue proximitydetected
info: StatlerWaldorfCorp.EventProcessor.Location.Redis
.RedisLocationCache[0]
      Using redis location cache - 127.0.0.1:6379,
allowAdmin=False,ssl=False,abortConnect=True,resolveDns=False
info: StatlerWaldorfCorp.EventProcessor.Queues.AMQP
.AMQPEventSubscriber[0]
      Subscribed to queue.
Hosting environment: Production
Content root path: (...)
Now listening on: http://0.0.0.0:5003
Application started. Press Ctrl+C to shut down.
```

The event processor has a number of dependencies, and you'll see a bunch of diagnostic information during startup that lets you know *where* it is attempting to find those dependencies.

At this point you should have the microservices and servers listed in Table 6-3 running (the italicized servers are third-party apps not written in this book).

Table 6-3. Event Sourcing sample processes

Service	Docker image	Port
RabbitMQ	`rabbitmq:3.6.6`	5672
Redis Cache	`redis:3.2.6`	6379
Team service	`dotnetcoreservices/teamservice`	5001
Location reporter	`dotnetcoreservices/locationreporter`	5002
Event processor	`dotnetcoreservices/es-eventprocessor`	5003
Reality service (optional)	`dotnetcoreservices/es-reality`	5004

If your workstation is anything like mine, this kind of workload running on a laptop's small memory footprint can grind it to a halt. If you find yourself in a crunch for resources, you should try using `dotnet run` for all of the .NET Core services built for this book and just leaving Redis and RabbitMQ for Docker.

Submitting Sample Data

First of all, if you have made it through to this point in the chapter, then congratulations and thank you for sticking with it! There is a lot of material in this chapter—a lot of code, and a ton of concepts that might have been new to you.

The reward now comes at the hand of your favorite REST client. All the samples in the book were tested with the Postman plug-in for Chrome, but you can use the *curl* command-line application or any other tool for sending custom HTTP payloads to services.

Use the following steps to exercise the entire Event Sourcing/CQRS system from end to end:

1. Issue a POST to `http://localhost:5001/teams` to create a new team. Refer to the source code in earlier chapters for the format, but the fields in the JSON that you'll need are `id` and `name`. Make sure you keep the GUID for the newly created team handy.
2. Issue a POST to `http://localhost:5001/teams/<new guid>/members` to add a member to the team. Make sure you keep the GUID for the new member handy.
3. Issue a POST to `http://localhost:5002/api/members/<member guid>/loca tionreports`. A location report requires the following fields: `ReportID`, `Lati tude`, `Longitude`, `Origin`, `ReportID`, and `MemberID`.
4. Watch the location report being converted to a `MemberLocationReportedEvent` and placed on the appropriate queue (the default is `memberlocationrecorded`). If you need some reference coordinates for latitude and longitude, you can find

several of them in the `GpsUtilityTest` class in the event processor unit test project.

5. Repeat step 3 a few times for locations that are far away from each other that will not trigger a proximity detected event.

6. Repeat step 2 to create a new member that belongs to the same team as your first test member.

7. Now repeat step 3 for this second team member at a location within a few kilometers of the most recently supplied location for the first team member.

8. You should now be able to see a new message in the `proximitydetected` queue (you can use the RabbitMQ management plug-in to view the queues without having to write code).

9. Either query the Redis cache directly or talk to the reality service to see the most up-to-date locations for members.

After having done this manually a few times, most teams building applications like this will then immediately devote some time to automating this process. Ideally you would automate the deployment of all of these services into an integration testing environment with a tool like `docker compose` or by creating deployments to Kubernetes or some other container scheduling environment.

The test script would then make all of the REST calls mentioned previously (probably many, many more of them) and then, when the test run is finished, assert that the right number of proximity detections showed up with the right values.

I recommend doing this as frequently as possible, either nightly or some time after the most recent check-in. Test suites like this will not only help prepare you for running in production, but will give you a baseline and alert you when new code causes a regression failure.

Summary

Code-wise, this chapter didn't introduce anything all that powerful or complex. It did, however, introduce several architectural concepts designed to allow multiple microservices to collaborate in support of an application that can scale elastically and react to internet-scale throughput.

Treating a system as *event sourced* has consequences—good and bad. In this chapter we built out a sample system that accepts commands requesting that a member's location be recorded. The command system then translates, augments, and ultimately injects events to be handled by an event processor. The event processor is responsible for detecting proximity events and emitting those to allow the rest of the system to notify team members when they are near each other.

ES/CQRS certainly will not solve all of your problems. In some situations it is clearly overkill, and in others it might not be enough. There are also many third-party products that allow data to flow through a system in a very ES-like fashion. Having built your own custom Event Sourcing suite of services, you should now know how these products work and, more importantly, why people choose to use them.

Throughout the chapter I recommended a few things that might make for useful reader exercises. I strongly recommend that you do these exercises, if for no other reason than to further build your muscle memory for building cloud-native, scalable services in ASP.NET Core.

CHAPTER 7

Building an ASP.NET Core Web Application

It is generally accepted that microservices are standalone applications that often expose RESTful APIs over HTTP(S). We've also seen microservices that are message-driven in nature and don't expose RESTful APIs, but rather operate by receiving and publishing messages.

Another type of microservice is a web application. This might seem like an odd assertion to those of you who have spent some time maintaining bloated, legacy web app monoliths. However, I believe that, when built properly, a web application is nothing more than a microservice that has an explicit contract to expose HTML over some subset of its endpoints.

In this chapter we'll take a look at how ASP.NET Core allows us to build web applications, but we'll examine this functionality with an eye toward how we can build high-performance, scalable, highly available web applications designed to thrive in the cloud rather than simply using a new technology to build an upgraded version of a legacy monolith.

All of the code for this chapter can be found in the GitHub repository (*https:// github.com/microservices-aspnetcore/webapp*).

ASP.NET Core Basics

In this section of the chapter we're going to take a tour of the basics of building web applications with ASP.NET Core. This will look very familiar to people who have built applications based on the Open Web Interface for .NET (OWIN) in the past and may look very alien to readers coming from a purely Web Forms–based development background.

A *lot* of what you'll see in this section should also look very familiar to you if you've been building the code samples for this book up until this point. There is a very noticeable (and intentional) overlap between defining routes and controllers for microservices and doing the same for view-based web applications.

Those of you with experience building .NET applications in the past might remember how difficult it was to migrate from one project template to another. For example, you couldn't start with a console application and then magically convert it into a web application. You'd have to copy out all of your useful code and paste it into a newly created project from the appropriate template. This problem plagued and irritated developers and thankfully no longer exists in the world of .NET Core.

In this chapter we're going to start with a command-line application and we'll finish with a fully functioning web app, without once using a template, scaffolding, or a wizard. Of course, Visual Studio wizards will make things easier and you can use them if you wish, but I'm going to show you how to do it by hand to stick to our approach of using the smallest amount of code to solve any given problem.

If you're interested in seeing the type of scaffolding Microsoft provides out of the box, you can type `dotnet new mvc --auth none`.

For the rest of this section, we'll start from scratch so you can see clearly how to get from a truly empty application to the autogenerated scaffolding.

If you recall from the first "hello world" sample we built in Chapter 1, we initially get a *Program.cs* file that contains the following code after we issue a `dotnet new console` command:

```
public class Program
{
    public static void Main(string[] args)
    {
        Console.WriteLine("Hello World!");
    }
}
```

We then modified the *Program.cs* file to add configuration support as well as enable the Kestrel web server, as shown here:

```
public static void Main(string[] args)
{
    var config = new ConfigurationBuilder()
                    .AddCommandLine(args)
                    .Build();

    var host = new WebHostBuilder()
                .UseContentRoot(Directory.GetCurrentDirectory())
                .UseKestrel()
                .UseStartup<Startup>()
                .UseConfiguration(config)
```

```
            .Build();

    host.Run();
}
```

Note the use of the `UseContentRoot` method. We have to do this so that when the application starts it can find all of the supporting files, like the *.cshtml* files for views.

Next we added a `Startup` class that configures the default middleware that responds with "Hello, world!" to all HTTP requests:

```
public class Startup
{
    public Startup(IHostingEnvironment env)
    {
    }

    public void Configure(IApplicationBuilder app,
        IHostingEnvironment env, ILoggerFactory loggerFactory)
    {
        app.Run(async (context) =>
        {
            await context.Response.WriteAsync("Hello, world!");
        });
    }
}
```

We also added the following NuGet packages as dependencies for our project:

`Microsoft.AspNetCore`
   The basic building blocks for all ASP.NET applications.

`Microsoft.AspNetCore.Server.Kestrel`
   The Kestrel web server.

`Microsoft.Extensions.Configuration.CommandLine`
   Extensions for parsing command-line parameters. This will be required to change the port number on which our application runs via command-line argument.

At this point, we technically have a functioning ASP.NET web application, but it is really just simple middleware that does nothing of value. While we've already got plenty of experience with controller routing for our microservices, we're going to finally delve into the "M" and "V" aspects of MVC: the *model* and *view*.

With the simplified syntax of the project file, we can simply indicate that we want to use the Web SDK (`Microsoft.NET.Sdk.Web`) at the opening of the project file, and that saves us from having to explicitly declare certain dependencies:

```
<Project Sdk="Microsoft.NET.Sdk.Web">

  <PropertyGroup>
    <TargetFramework>netcoreapp1.1</TargetFramework>
  </PropertyGroup>

  <ItemGroup>
    <PackageReference Include="Microsoft.AspNetCore"
      Version="1.1.1" />
    <PackageReference Include="Microsoft.AspNetCore.Mvc"
      Version="1.1.2" />
    <PackageReference Include="Microsoft.AspNetCore.StaticFiles"
      Version="1.1.1" />
    <PackageReference Include="Microsoft.Extensions.Logging.Debug"
      Version="1.1.1" />
    <PackageReference Include="Microsoft.VisualStudio.Web.BrowserLink"
      Version="1.1.0" />
    <PackageReference Include="Microsoft.Extensions.Configuration"
      Version="1.1.1"/>
    <PackageReference
       Include="Microsoft.Extensions.Options.ConfigurationExtensions"
      Version="1.1.1"/>
    <PackageReference Include="Microsoft.Extensions.Configuration.Json"
      Version="1.1.1"/>
    <PackageReference Include="Microsoft.Extensions.Configuration.CommandLine"
      Version="1.1.1"/>
  </ItemGroup>

</Project>
```

Adding ASP.NET MVC Middleware

In this next section of the chapter we're going to talk about how to go from a simple console application that is using "hello world" middleware in conjunction with the Kestrel web server to the more familiar MVC middleware.

Let's enhance our existing sample by adding support for the MVC framework with the default routing scheme that we're familiar with. To do this, we simply replace the app.Use middleware configuration with the UseMvc extension in the Startup class, as shown in our new class (Example 7-1).

Example 7-1. Startup.cs

```
using Microsoft.AspNetCore.Builder;
using Microsoft.AspNetCore.Hosting;
using Microsoft.Extensions.Logging;
using Microsoft.Extensions.DependencyInjection;

namespace StatlerWaldorfCorp.WebApp
{
```

```
public class Startup
{
    public Startup(IHostingEnvironment env)
    {

    }

    public void ConfigureServices(IServiceCollection services) {
        services.AddMvc();
    }

    public void Configure(IApplicationBuilder app,
        IHostingEnvironment env, ILoggerFactory loggerFactory)
    {
        app.UseMvc(routes =>
        {
            routes.MapRoute("default",
             template:
               "{controller=Home}/{action=Index}/{id?}");
        });
    }
}
}
```

For this to work, we'll also need to add a dependency on the NuGet package `Microsoft.AspNetCore.Mvc`.

This is in keeping with .NET Core's modular philosophy. Everything we need is available *à la carte*, and we no longer need to rely on a single mammoth framework that includes mountains of code we'll never use.

The default route that we added should look familiar to you if you've done any ASP.NET MVC development in the past. Go ahead and run this application with the usual command-line tools (`dotnet restore`, `dotnet run`) and see what happens. You should simply get 404s on every possible route because we have no controllers.

Adding a Controller

We've seen controllers already throughout the book—it's how we've been exposing our RESTful APIs. We're going to create a default (home) controller that just returns some text, and we'll move on from there.

There are many areas within ASP.NET applications that are commonly referred to as "disputed areas," or areas in which conflict between developers and architects often arises. The role and size of controllers is one of those debates that will continue until the end of time, though my personal view on this is that controllers should be as small as possible.

Controllers should do the following and *nothing more*:

1. Accept input from HTTP requests.
2. Delegate the input to service classes that are written without regard for HTTP transport or JSON parsing.
3. Return an appropriate response code and body.

In other words, our controllers should be very, very small. They should do little more than wrap highly tested components that can operate outside the context of a web request if necessary.

To add a controller to our project, let's create a new folder called *Controllers* and put a class in it called HomeController (Example 7-2).

Example 7-2. HomeController.cs

```
using Microsoft.AspNetCore.Mvc;

namespace StatlerWaldorfCorp.Controllers
{
    public class HomeController : Controller
    {
        public string Index()
        {
            return "Hello World";
        }
    }
}
```

With the simple addition of this file, the route we created earlier will automatically pick up the existence of this controller and let us use it. If you run the app from the command line and hit the home URL (e.g., http://localhost:5000 or whatever port you're running on) you'll see the text "Hello World" in your browser.

Adding a Model

The role of the model is, as you might have guessed, to represent the data required by the controller and the view to present some form of interaction between the user and the application. This isn't a book on building ASP.NET MVC web applications (there are far more detailed references available), so we won't go into all of the things that you can do with models, like automatic validation and so on.

To keep things simple, in Example 7-3 we'll just create a model representing a simple stock quote (created in a new *Models* folder).

Example 7-3. StockQuote.cs

```
namespace StatlerWaldorfCorp.WebApp.Models
{
    public class StockQuote
    {
        public string Symbol { get; set; }
        public int Price { get; set; }
    }
}
```

A Note on Storing Currency Values in a Model

You might have noticed that I decided to represent the price in the stock quote as an integer. There are a number of reasons for this, but most of them stem from catastrophic system failures that have happened at two in the morning during a vacation. Most of the languages we use daily do a terrible job of preserving significant digits while doing "financial arithmetic" on decimals. A long-standing tradition is to do all the math on straight-up integers (where the last two digits are cents) and only convert the value into something that looks like dollars and cents when it finally reaches the end user.

Adding a View

Now that we've got a controller and a model, let's build a view to render that data to the user via server-side templating. Just like with the controller and the model, there is a default convention for locating the views that correspond to controllers.

For example, if we wanted to create a view for the HomeController's Index method, we would store that view as *Index.cshtml* in the *Views/Home* directory. Example 7-4 is a sample view that renders a stock quote model.

Example 7-4. Views/Home/Index.cshtml

```
<html>
<head>
    <title>Hello world</title>
</head>
<body>
    <h1>Hello World</h1>
    <div>
        <h2>Stock Quote</h2>
        <div>
            Symbol: @Model.Symbol<br/>
            Price: $@Model.Price<br/>
        </div>
    </div>
```

```
</body>
</html>
```

Now we can modify our home controller to render a view instead of returning simple text:

```
using Microsoft.AspNetCore.Mvc;
using System.Threading.Tasks;
using webapp.Models;

namespace webapp.Controllers
{
    public class HomeController : Controller
    {
        public async Task<IActionResult> Index()
        {
            var model = new StockQuote { Symbol = "HLLO",
                                         Price = 3200 };

            return View(model);
        }
    }
}
```

Of course it won't really be this easy, and if you go run the application now, you will probably get an HTTP 500 response. Since we're building a web application, we're definitely going to want to have stack traces of errors that show up, so we can add a line that invokes the UseDeveloperExceptionPage method to our Startup class, in the Configure method.

Here is our new and complete Startup class:

```
using Microsoft.AspNetCore.Builder;
using Microsoft.AspNetCore.Hosting;
using Microsoft.Extensions.Logging;
using Microsoft.Extensions.DependencyInjection;
using Microsoft.Extensions.Configuration;

namespace StatlerWaldorfCorp.WebApp
{
    public class Startup
    {
        public Startup(IHostingEnvironment env)
        {
            var builder = new ConfigurationBuilder()
                .SetBasePath(env.ContentRootPath)
                .AddEnvironmentVariables();

            Configuration = builder.Build();
        }

        public IConfiguration Configuration { get; set; }
```

```
public void ConfigureServices(IServiceCollection services)
{
    services.AddMvc();
}

public void Configure(IApplicationBuilder app,
    IHostingEnvironment env, ILoggerFactory loggerFactory)
{
    loggerFactory.AddConsole();
    loggerFactory.AddDebug();

    app.UseDeveloperExceptionPage();
    app.UseMvc(routes =>
    {
     routes.MapRoute("default",
       template: "{controller=Home}/{action=Index}/{id?}");
    });
    app.UseStaticFiles();
}
  }
}
```

For a complete list of all of the dependencies required for the ASP.NET application, take a look at the *.csproj* file in the GitHub repository (*https://github.com/ microservices-aspnetcore/webapp*).

With this new `Startup` class, we should be able to do a `dotnet restore` and a `dotnet run` to start our application. Hitting the home page should combine our controller, our view, and our model to produce a rendered HTML page for the browser, as shown in Figure 7-1.

Figure 7-1. ASP.NET Core model, view, and controller in action

Invoking REST APIs from JavaScript

Historically, ASP.NET applications were written such that a request gets submitted to the server, the server does a ton of work, and the user is presented with prerendered HTML. The dynamic portions of the page were all taken care of server-side through the use of templating.

In the past this was done either through legacy Web Forms (*.asmx* files) or through the type of rendering we've shown so far in this chapter—MVC templating. Both of these types of server-side templating and rendering are considered "old school" by most web application developers these days. Today, the most common type of web application is a single-page application (SPA) that just loads up in the browser and communicates with one or more APIs—no server-side templating is involved.

In a single-page app, the server renders an HTML page along with links to include a mountain of JavaScript. The JavaScript loads in the client browser and then interacts with a RESTful API exposed by the web application in order to provide the end users with the type of experience they've come to expect from modern web and mobile applications.

Throughout the book so far we've seen a number of examples of how to expose a RESTful API, so it should be a pretty easy exercise to add an API endpoint to the project we're building in this chapter. First, let's create an API endpoint to use by adding a new controller, the `ApiController` (Example 7-5).

Example 7-5. Controllers/ApiController.cs

```
using Microsoft.AspNetCore.Mvc;
using webapp.Models;

namespace webapp.Controllers
{
    [Route("api/test")]
    public class ApiController : Controller
    {
        [HttpGet]
        public IActionResult GetTest()
        {
            return this.Ok(new StockQuote
            {
                Symbol = "API",
                Price = 9999
            });
        }
    }
}
```

If you run the application again right now, then you can hit *http://localhost:5000/api/test* with your favorite browser and you'll see a JSON payload (with lowercased property names by default) that looks like this:

```
{
    "symbol" : "API",
    "price" : 9999
}
```

This represents a typical scenario where our single-page app (whether we've written it in Angular 1, Angular 2, React/Flux, or whatever framework is hip and trendy at the time) will make JavaScript client calls.

Again, the controller exposing the API should be *simple* and *small*. These API controllers should delegate all the real work to other components and, ideally, those components, and are delegating to backing services in our ecosystem.

The Single Responsibility Principle and Services

We should never need to push a new version of the GUI portion of our application (the ASP.NET MVC application and the facade API layer that comes with it) as a result of changing the implementation of some core piece of business logic or data functionality. Our GUI is a microservice, and should abide by the same rules about "what is micro?" to which all our other services adhere.

Now that we've got an API to consume, let's modify our single view so that it grabs some JavaScript to consume it (Example 7-6).

Example 7-6. Views/Index.cshtml (modified)

```
<html>
<head>
    <title>Hello world</title>
    <script src="https://ajax.googleapis.com/ajax/libs/jquery/1.10.2/jquery.min.js">
    </script>
    <script src="/wwwroot/Scripts/hello.js"></script>
</head>
<body>
    <h1>Hello World</h1>
    <div>
        <h2>Stock Quote</h2>
        <div>
            Symbol: @Model.Symbol<br/>
            Price: $@Model.Price<br/>
        </div>
    </div>
    <br/>
    <div>
```

```
    <p class="quote-symbol">The Symbol is </p>
    <p class="quote-price">The price is $</p>
  </div>
</body>
</html>
```

Note that I've decided to include JQuery here as well as a new script, *hello.js*. We're going to add this to a new directory called *wwwroot* by convention. The goal is to keep the samples simple and focused squarely on our goals for the book—building services for the cloud. We're hoping to stay out of the religious war that is the battle of client-side JavaScript frameworks.

Our *hello.js* script just waits for the page to be ready and then consumes our API and appends the result of the data call to the new paragraph elements we've added to the page. The source code for *hello.js* is shown in Example 7-7.

Example 7-7. wwwroot/Scripts/hello.js

```
$(document).ready(function () {
    $.ajax({
        url: "/api/test"
    }).then(function (data) {
        $('.quote-symbol').append(data.symbol);
        $('.quote-price').append(data.price);
    });
});
```

This is just some straightforward jQuery that makes an Ajax call to our API endpoint. The object that comes back will have the `symbol` and `price` properties, which we'll use to append to the new paragraph elements.

The static files, like our image assets, stylesheets, and JavaScript files, are all made available to browsers through the use of the `UseStaticFiles` extension method we used in our `Startup` class. Without this, attempts to access files we've stored in the *wwwroot* directory would return a 404 Not Found error code to the browser.

We've established the content root (you can see it show up in the debug output when you run the application) with the call to `SetBasePath` in the `Startup` class's constructor, which allows our static files to default to the *wwwroot* directory. If we wanted a different relative path we could configure it as an option in the extension method.

Now when we launch the application, we should get what we're expecting when we try and load *http://localhost:5000*. The output is shown in Figure 7-2.

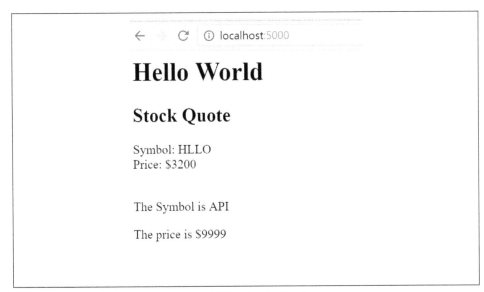

Figure 7-2. JavaScript consuming an API endpoint inside a view

Building Cloud-Native Web Applications

In this chapter we've spent most of our time and effort going through the low-level details of starting with a console application in .NET Core and progressively adding the smallest amount of code possible to iteratively reach a point where we have built something that resembles an ASP.NET web application.

Giving you the technical details of building a web application is not the ultimate goal of this book. The ultimate goal of this book is to teach you how to use .NET Core to build powerful, fast, highly scalable, resilient microservices that thrive in the cloud. The remaining chapters of this book will be dedicated to implementing cloud-native patterns and the concerns of building applications that are "good citizens" in a cloud-native ecosystem.

Keeping in mind that a web GUI is nothing more than a specialized form of microservice, there are some guidelines inspired by my *Beyond the Twelve-Factor App* (*http://oreil.ly/2vpkhpY*) mini-book (O'Reilly) that have specific ramifications for ASP.NET Core developers, and they are outlined in this section for you to read and swear you will adopt under penalty of bloody, violent death prior to continuing with the rest of the book.

API First

When building applications that consume services, you cannot build that application unless you know the public contract for that service's API. There are a number of technologies available to us, like API Blueprint, that allow for the publication and documentation of APIs.

Regardless of the tool you use, adopting the discipline of always starting at the seams of your services by agreeing on fixed public APIs will do your organization a ton of good and save you a mountain of headaches in the long run.

Later in the book we will discuss some techniques for dynamically discovering the location (URL) of backing services, a problem common to nearly every organization building microservices.

Configuration

So far we haven't seen that much configuration other than the occasional database connection string or URL of a backing service. When we move toward real production pipelines for continuously delivering microservices in multiple environments as well as resilient green/blue delivery of applications visible to the outside world, the need to store our configuration outside the application becomes a mandate for all teams.

In the mini-book I refer to this need by suggesting that you treat code, configuration, and credentials as volatile substances that explode when combined. Later in this book we'll take a look at a number of tools available to you for taking configuration data that might otherwise have lived in a *web.config* or *appsettings.json* file and externalizing it somewhere more secure and robust, ideally in a location that audits all changes and has multiple layers of security.

Logging

> *In the cloud, no one can hear you log to disk.*
>
> —Kevin Hoffman, author

The filesystem on which your application is running in the cloud needs to be treated as though it is ephemeral. At any time, the disk supporting your application can be taken away, and that instance of your application torn down and restarted on another coast, country, or even continent.

As a result, you cannot rely on the existence or examination of physical files to troubleshoot your application and analyze activity.

Nearly all PaaS solutions advise application developers to log all informational messages to stdout (or, as .NET developers view it, the console). The PaaS will then be responsible for collecting those logs and shipping them off to some endpoint where you can then perform all the aggregation, historical archiving, and analysis you require.

This essentially simplifies the job of a service and application developer. We don't need complex logging systems or file rollover and purging logic embedded in our applications. We just write to stdout or stderr and leave the grunt work to some other component of our overall topology.

Session State

Just as we needed to change our mindsets and some of our code and configuration when we went from running a single instance of our application to running multiple instances on a physical or virtual "web farm," so too do we need to change our thinking when running in the cloud.

This essentially bars us from using in-memory session state for our cloud-native web applications. We must use an out-of-process provider. Whether it's the easy-to-use and favorite wizard target of the SQL Server session state or a different technology like Redis or Gemfire, the requirement remains the same: if we're deploying our application to the cloud, it cannot use in-memory session state.

Carrying the state discussion even further, we should *never* store anything in memory that will last beyond the lifetime of an individual HTTP request. If something needs to live longer than that, it should probably be the responsibility of a backing service or an out-of-process cache.

Data Protection

One of the things that is often done implicitly on behalf of our applications is data protection. Middleware that we use will encrypt and decrypt data for us without ever really getting in our way.

This works great, and we rarely have to worry about it...until we try and run our applications in the cloud.

Let's assume that some bit of state is encrypted by an instance (call it instance 0) of our application and returned to the client. The next time the client calls our app, it is directed at instance 1 (a very common round-robin routing protocol used when instances of an application are sitting behind a reverse proxy or load balancer in the cloud). The client hands over the encrypted data, but the instance of our application or service is unable to decrypt it. Why? What went wrong?

What often happens is that the application, or some piece of middleware working on behalf of the application, creates a brand new encryption key and stores it *locally, on the local filesystem*. Remembering that storing things on the local filesystem is a quick way to screw up all kinds of cloud-native behavior, we know that instance 1 will never be able to see data written to the filesystem of instance 0, even if they happen to be on the same virtual machine, because PaaS solutions deal almost exclusively with isolated containers.

So now we need to keep in mind that if we're going to involve data protection, we need to apply the same out-of-process mentality to the storage of keys. We need to use an off-the-shelf key vault, a cloud-based key vault, or roll our own solution with storage like Redis or another database.

This hammers home one of our key points: that working in a cloud-native manner is far more of a shift in process and paradigm than it is in simple tooling.

Backing Services

I've said it before and I'll say it again—we never have the luxury of building a single service in a vacuum. Up to this point in the book, we've been "discovering" our backing services the hard way, either through hacks, hardcoding URLs, or sticking them in configuration files.

The location and nature of our backing services should be exposed to us through the environment, and never through configuration or code (see the previous comment about *credentials*, *code*, and *configuration* being volatile substances that explode when combined).

I'll show you a number of ways to deal with backing service discovery and monitoring throughout the book, and there's an upcoming chapter dedicated entirely to the topic of dynamic service discovery with a Netflix OSS tool called Eureka.

Environment Parity

At some point in the past, the .NET developer community of which we were proud members decided that it would be a fantastic thing to allow for the use of multiple *Web.config* files, essentially one per environment.

We could have a developer workstation config file, a shared development environment config file, one for staging, one for quality assurance, one for user acceptance testing, and finally one or more files for production.

We'd end up with a solution that contained a *Web.DEV.config* file, plus *Web.QA.config*, *Web.UAT.config*, and so on. This solution was so ingrained in how everyone did things that Visual Studio's Solution Explorer even had native support for this notion, and would collapse all of the environment-specific configuration files up under a single *Web.config* file.

This is now considered an anti-pattern. This is not externalizing your configuration or getting your configuration data from the environment itself. This is violating the cardinal rule of allowing code, credentials, and configuration to all touch each other.

The only configuration values that should be checked into source control with your main application code are values that never change across environments; values that, when they change, actually warrant the release of a new version of your application.

In most real-world cases, applying this rule reduces the size of an application's configuration file to either nothing, or some really tiny artifact.

In terms of how this impacts the average .NET Core developer, it means that directly or indirectly, your application must invoke both the `AddCommandLine` method and the `AddEnvironmentVariables` method during startup.

You also need to store environment-specific configuration data external to the application, and we will devote an entire upcoming chapter to discussing one technique for solving this problem.

Port Binding

Port binding refers to your application being a passive participant in the acquisition of a port on which to run the app. In other words, the PaaS environment needs to tell your application which port has been reserved for it within the isolated container currently hosting your application.

This port can (and almost always does) change from one startup to another for your application. Legacy code like Windows Communication Foundation port bindings that specifically try and grab actual ports on a virtual or physical machine are incompatible with the idea of container-based port mappings.

To support container-assigned ports in any cloud environment, your application needs to allow for command-line override of the server URLs, with the `server.urls` property, as shown here:

```
dotnet run --server.urls=http://0.0.0.0:90210
```

PaaS platforms often make available the port to which your application must bind as an environment variable called `PORT`. This means your application will need to ingest environment variables and make them available inside the `IConfiguration` instance injected into your app. To do this, you'll need to make sure your app invokes both `AddCommandLine` and `AddEnvironmentVariables`.

Whether you're using `docker compose`, deploying to Kubernetes, or using AWS, Azure, or GCP, your app will need to be able to accept whatever port number has been predetermined for it in order to play nice in the cloud.

Telemetry

Monitoring your application in the cloud is vastly different from how you monitor it when it is up close and you can attach all kinds of debuggers and diagnostic equipment to it. This applies to ASP.NET legacy applications as well as .NET Core services.

I'm not going to recommend which monitoring tools you should use. Rather, I'll instead ask that you try and view your applications as satellites that are going to be launched into orbit when deployed to your favorite PaaS. Viewing them this way will guide the choices you make for monitoring tools as well as the type of information you emit to `stdout` and `stderr` logs (knowing you'll have aggregate access to those via yet another tool, like Splunk or SumoLogic).

Authentication and Authorization

Securing applications and services in the cloud shouldn't be all that different from securing legacy web applications running in your own data centers. Unfortunately, the luxuries afforded to us by running applications that we know are physically close to our center of operations let us take a number of shortcuts.

The easiest shortcut for intranet applications is to simply embrace Windows authentication and pull the user's information from a Kerberos-based browser identity challenge. This isn't going to work when our services are running on an ephemeral operating system that is probably not Windows (since we're using .NET Core) and, even if it was Windows, isn't joined to a particular workgroup or domain that would allow for normal Windows authentication to work.

Fear not; there is an entire forthcoming chapter dedicated to the topic of securing web applications and microservices in the cloud, so we'll have plenty of examples on how to solve this problem.

Summary

In this chapter we learned that an ASP.NET Core MVC application is really nothing more than a microservice with a specialized form of middleware that knows how to render templated HTML on endpoints in addition to simple text and JSON endpoints.

The purpose behind this wasn't to teach you how to build fancy web applications; it was instead to show you how to progress from a console application to a web application without the use of a wizard or special IDE-based template. Knowing how to add the necessary dependencies, configuration, and middleware really illustrates how little difference there is between a web application and a microservice.

We also discussed a number of problems and issues inherent in building apps and services destined for the cloud. At this point you should be ready for the rest of the book, which will immediately dive into the deep end of the cloud-native pool to start addressing the problems that arise as part of building an entire ecosystem of services rather than simply building a single service in isolation.

CHAPTER 8

Service Discovery

Up to this point in the book, we have discussed the concepts and code required to build basic microservices, configure and consume backing services, talk to databases, and build web applications. We've even spent a great deal of time and effort discussing the Event Sourcing and CQRS patterns and how they can be applied to build massive-scale applications out of a suite of related microservices.

In this chapter we're going to continue to build on the idea that we don't simply build single services in a vacuum; that everything we build is consumed by or consumes other services.

To keep the configuration and management of large numbers of services as simple as possible, I'm going to introduce the concept of *service discovery*.

Refresher on Cloud-Native Factors

Before we get into the details of service discovery, I thought it would be worth a quick refresher on some of the original *twelve factors* of cloud-native applications that are important and relevant to the sample we'll be building: *external configuration* and *backing services*.

External Configuration

As discussed throughout this book and on the original Twelve-Factor App website (*https://12factor.net/config*), properly handling configuration is key to building applications that thrive in the cloud.

Let's start with a review of what it looks like when we aren't properly externalizing our configuration. How many times have you seen (or written) code that looks like this in your application?

```
using (var httpClient = new HttpClient())
{
    httpClient.BaseAddress = new Uri("http://foo.bar/baz");
    ...
}
```

The address of the backing service is *hardcoded* in your application code. When you commit this to your version-control system, the URL is sitting there, unaltered. This is even more problematic if you've embedded credentials in the URL. This value can't easily change from one environment to the next, and you have to recompile every time you decide to change hostnames.

When people see how problematic this is, they often move the URL out of the C# code and into a *web.config* file or a *web.<environment>.config* environment-specific configuration file. These are then checked into revision control repositories, and we naively think our problems have been solved.

Unfortunately, *any configuration checked into source control might as well be hardcoded.* You should consider any values sitting in a configuration file (*web.config*, *appsettings.json*, whatever) as *part of your code*. As such, credentials and URLs and other environment-specific settings should *never* be included in these files.

The next logical step in this evolutionary process is to move the URLs and credentials out of configuration files, out of C# files, and into *environment variables*. Written this way, our code makes it obvious what configuration parameters it needs in order to function, but it leaves the responsibility of supplying those values up to the environment.

Whether we're using raw virtual machines, Docker images, or a higher-level PaaS, we should always have ways to securely inject environment variables into our applications.

Backing Services

I've harped on this concept enough in this book that you're probably getting sick of seeing it. It is actually worth repeating this point, though everything your application needs must be treated as though it is a backing service.

Whether you need binary storage for files, a database, another web service, a queue service, or anything else, the thing you need should be *loosely coupled*, and *configured from the environment*.

There are two ways to *bind* a resource that is a backing service: static binding and dynamic (runtime) binding. So far in this book we've only discussed static binding.

Statically bound resources

Statically bound resources are the ones we've been using in all of our sample code up to this point. While we've been careful to allow for environment-based replacement of default values to connect to databases, web services, and queuing services, this binding is fixed by the environment.

Whether defined by automation tools or DevOps personnel, the binding between the service and its resource is persistent and made available to the application *at start time*, and it *does not change*.

While this certainly satisfies the external configuration requirement for cloud-native applications, it might not be flexible enough for your needs. Maybe you want something a little more dynamic and powerful.

Dynamically bound resources

A dynamically bound resource is one where the binding occurs at *runtime*. Moreover, this binding is not fixed and can actually change at runtime between requests to the application.

In addition to freeing up the developers of the application from a little bit of complexity, it also allows for even looser coupling. This dynamic, loose runtime coupling between apps and bound resources facilitates more advanced functionality like failover, load balancing, fault tolerance—all with no visible impact to the application code.

Dynamic resource binding will be the focus of the rest of this chapter.

> **Dynamic Binding May Require One Static Binding**
>
> Dynamic resource binding is often managed through a broker or some central point of management that keeps a catalog of services. For this to work, your application needs to know how to find the broker/manager. This is usually done, oddly enough, through a static resource binding. It is for this reason and additional complexity that you should evaluate the number of services you have and how much you need the dynamic binding before you implement discovery.

Introducing Netflix Eureka

In order to discover services at runtime, you're going to need something that serves as a *service registry*; a central catalog of services. This registry and the features it offers can vary from product to product, but by and large most service registries provide at the basic level a list of services, metadata about the services, and their endpoint(s).

You may also be able to get status or heartbeat information to help you determine if a service that claims to be online really is online.

Netflix's infrastructure is predominantly run on top of Amazon Web Services. As you might imagine from the size and complexity of the product Netflix offers and the sheer volume of concurrently connected customers, Netflix's microservice ecosystem is *vast*, to say the least.

While AWS has plenty of functionality available for load balancing at the edge, and it has a naming service (Route 53) that can function as a full DNS service, neither of these services are entirely appropriate for mid-tier service naming, registry, and load balancing.

With Eureka, Netflix built its own internal product to manage the service registry that allowed for failover and load balancing. It's still using a far more advanced version of this product internally, but to our gain and enjoyment, Netflix has open sourced the core of its functionality. You can find this code on GitHub (*https://github.com/Netflix/eureka*).

From a developer's perspective, your service code interacts with a Eureka server by registering itself when it starts up. If you need to discover and consume other backing services, then you can ask the Eureka server for some or all of the service registry. Your service also emits a *heartbeat* to the Eureka service at some interval (usually 30 seconds). If your service fails to send a heartbeat to Eureka after some number of intervals, it will be taken out of the registry.

If there are multiple instances of your service running, and consumers of your service are talking to Eureka to find your service, then they will stop getting the URL of the service that was taken out of the registry due to heartbeat failure and will simply refer to the service instances that are up and running.

Figure 8-1, available on the Eureka at a Glance (*https://github.com/Netflix/eureka/wiki/Eureka-at-a-glance*) documentation page on GitHub, illustrates how Netflix has deployed Eureka and how it expects it to be deployed in a typical organization.

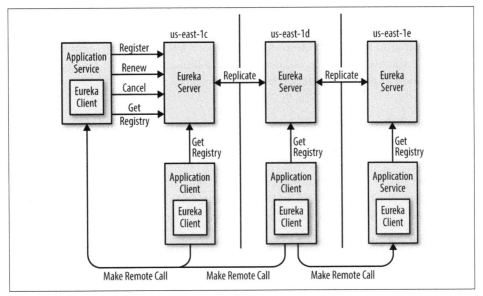

Figure 8-1. Typical Eureka deployment within AWS

Eureka is a powerful product with a lot of features that we simply don't have the room to discuss at length in this book. I encourage you to read up on the documentation and more advanced features if you think your project or organization might benefit from these features.

Eureka is also not the only player in the service registry and discovery game. There are a number of other companies and products available that provide everything from the bare-bones service registry to more full-featured registry, discovery, and fault-tolerance functionality.

Just a few of the more popular products are:

etcd

> Pronounced "etsee-dee," etcd (*https://coreos.com/etcd*) is a low-level distributed key-value store accessible via HTTP. As such, you actually need to bolt on additional tools to make it serve as a service discovery and registry mechanism. You'll often see tools like etcd combined with registrator and confd to bring them up to par with other products like Consul and Eureka.

Consul

> Consul (*https://www.consul.io*) is full-featured service discovery tool that and also provides a key-value store for configuration. It uses a gossip protocol to form clusters.

Marathon

> Marathon (*https://mesosphere.github.io/marathon/*) is a full-fledged container orchestration system for Mesos and DC/OS. As such, it does *a lot* more than just service discovery. Service discovery is more like a free benefit you get by using Marathon as your container orchestration layer.

ZooKeeper

> Originally born of the Hadoop project, ZooKeeper (*https://zookeeper.apache.org*) is one of the oldest of this family of products and is mature and stable, though many argue it is showing its age and you may be better off with other products.

If you want to try out Eureka (and use it for the code later in this chapter) without the commitment of having to build it from source or install a full copy on a server, you can just run it from a docker hub image, as shown in the following command:

```
$ docker run -p 8080:8080 -d --name eureka \
    -d netflixoss/eureka:1.3.1
```

This will run a default, *nonproduction* copy of the server in your Docker virtual machine and map port 8080 from inside the container to your local machine. This means, assuming port 8080 is available, that when you statically bind an application to this Eureka server, you'll use the URL `http://localhost:8080/eureka`.

Discovering and Advertising ASP.NET Core Services

Now that we've spent some time discussing the concepts and real-world scenarios that drive the need for service discovery, let's take a look at some sample code that communicates with a Eureka server to do just that.

In our somewhat contrived sample, we're going to be building a suite of services that support an ecommerce application. The edge service is responsible for exposing a product catalog. This catalog has standard API endpoints for exposing a list of products as well as product details. There is also an inventory service that is responsible for exposing the real-time status of physical inventory. The product service will need to discover the inventory service and make calls to it in order to return enriched data when asked for product details.

To keep things simple, our sample has just these two services. In a real, large-scale application that supports mobile clients, and internal customers, communicates with multiple third-party vendors, and orchestrates multiple data flows, you could see communication between dozens or hundreds of services. As you saw in Netflix's diagram earlier in the chapter, the need to provide high availability, failover, and load balancing across regions and within regions is satisfied by multiple installations of Eureka.

Registering a Service

The first part of our sample is the inventory service, a service that needs to be dynamically discovered at runtime to provide real-time inventory status.

If you felt like it, you could communicate directly with the Eureka API yourself as it's just a set of RESTful API calls. However, it's always good to look around and see if someone else is actively maintaining a solution to the problem at hand. This saves you the trouble of reinventing the wheel.

In our case, the Steeltoe project (*https://github.com/steeltoeoss*) maintains a number of client libraries for Netflix OSS projects, including Eureka. While the samples throughout this chapter will rely on the Steeltoe discovery client library, I strongly encourage you to go looking for other libraries as you read this. If you find one that suits your needs better, by all means use that one. At the time this book was written, Steeltoe was basically the only game in town for .NET Core discovery clients.

The Steeltoe library allows us to supply some configuration information using the standard .NET Core configuration system. The key things that we need to declare are the name of our application (this is how it will be identified in the registry) and the URL pointing to the Eureka server, as shown here:

```
{
  "spring": {
    "application": {
      "name":  "inventory"
    }
  },
  "eureka": {
    "client": {
      "serviceUrl": "http://localhost:8080/eureka/",
      "shouldRegisterWithEureka": true,
      "shouldFetchRegistry": false,
      "validate_certificates": false
    },
    "instance": {
      "port": 5000
    }
  }
}
```

Another key part of this configuration is the value `shouldRegisterWithEureka`. If we want our service to be *discoverable* then we must choose `true` here. The next setting, `shouldFetchRegistry`, indicates whether we want to *discover* other services.

Put another way, we need to indicate whether we're consuming registry information or producing it—or both. Our inventory service wants to be discovered and does not need to discover anything else; therefore it will not fetch the registry, but it will register itself.

We'll build our configuration the same way we always do, ensuring that we load the *appsettings.json* file with our discovery client configuration:

```
var builder = new ConfigurationBuilder()
                .SetBasePath(env.ContentRootPath)
                .AddJsonFile("appsettings.json", optional: false,
                reloadOnChange: true)
                .AddEnvironmentVariables();

Configuration = builder.Build();
```

Then we'll use Steeltoe's `AddDiscoveryClient` extension method in our `Startup` class's `ConfigureServices` method:

```
services.AddDiscoveryClient(Configuration);
```

Finally, we just need to add a call to `UseDiscoveryClient` in our `Configure` method:

```
app.UseDiscoveryClient();
```

That's it! Since we're not actually consuming any services from inside the inventory service, we're pretty much done. Obviously we need controllers and an API and to return some fabricated data, but we've covered all of those techniques extensively throughout the book. If you want to look at the rest of the code, just grab the `ecommerce-inventory` repository from the book's GitHub (*https://github.com/ microservices-aspnetcore/ecommerce-inventory*).

We will come back to this service later, after we've created our next service.

Discovering and Consuming Services

With a service ready to be discovered, let's turn our attention to the next service we're going to build: the *catalog*. This service exposes a product catalog and then augments product detail requests by querying the inventory service.

The key difference between this service and the others we've built so far is that this one will dynamically discover the URL of the catalog service at runtime.

We'll configure the client almost the same way we configured the inventory service:

```
"spring": {
  "application": {
    "name": "catalog"
  }
},
"eureka": {
  "client": {
    "serviceUrl": "http://localhost:8080/eureka/",
    "shouldRegisterWithEureka": false,
    "shouldFetchRegistry": true,
    "validate_certificates":  false
```

```
        }
    }
```

The difference is that the catalog service doesn't need to register (since it does not need to be discovered), and it should fetch the registry so it can discover the inventory service.

Your patience going through this chapter is about to be rewarded. Take a look at the code for the `HttpInventoryClient` class, the class responsible for consuming the inventory service:

```
using StatlerWaldorfCorp.EcommerceCatalog.Models;
using Steeltoe.Discovery.Client;
using System.Threading.Tasks;
using System.Net.Http;
using Newtonsoft.Json;

namespace StatlerWaldorfCorp.EcommerceCatalog.InventoryClient
{
    public class HttpInventoryClient : IInventoryClient
    {
        private DiscoveryHttpClientHandler handler;
        private const string INVENTORYSERVICE_URL_BASE =
            "http://inventory/api/skustatus/";

        public HttpInventoryClient(IDiscoveryClient client)
        {
            this.handler = new DiscoveryHttpClientHandler(client);
        }

        private HttpClient CreateHttpClient()
        {
            return new HttpClient(this.handler, false);
        }

        public async Task<StockStatus> GetStockStatusAsync(int sku) {
            StockStatus stockStatus = null;

            using (HttpClient client = this.CreateHttpClient())
            {
                var result =
                    await client.GetStringAsync(
                        INVENTORYSERVICE_URL_BASE + sku.ToString());
                stockStatus =
                    JsonConvert.DeserializeObject<StockStatus>(
                        result);
            }

            return stockStatus;
        }
    }
}
```

The .NET Core `HttpClient` class has a variant of its constructor that lets you pass in an instance of your own `HttpHandler`. The `DiscoveryHttpClientHandler` provided by Steeltoe is responsible for swapping the service name in your URL with the actual, runtime-discovered URL. This is what allows our code to rely on a URL like `http://inventory/api/skustatus`, which can then be converted by Steeltoe and Eureka to something like `http://inventory.myapps.mydomain.com/api/skustatus`.

Check out the full sample code for the catalog service (*http://bit.ly/2vlcaqV*) and the inventory service (*http://bit.ly/2wjtlh8*).

To run the inventory service, the catalog service, and Eureka all at the same time on your computer, use the following steps.

First, start the Eureka server:

```
$ docker run -p 8080:8080 -d --name eureka \
    -d netflixoss/eureka:1.3.1
```

Then start the inventory service on port 5001:

```
$ cd <inventory service>
$ dotnet run --server.urls=http://0.0.0.0:5001
```

Depending on your computer and what's installed, you might see an error message like this:

```
Steeltoe.Discovery.Eureka.DiscoveryClient[0]
    Register failed, Exception:
System.PlatformNotSupportedException: The libcurl library in use (7.51.0)
and its SSL backend ("SecureTransport")
do not support custom handling of certificates.
A libcurl built with OpenSSL is required.
```

If this happens and you cannot update your version of `curl` with `openssl` and are still having trouble on your Mac, then you can just run the Linux version of the inventory service right from the book's published docker hub image.

This particular problem adds ammunition to my argument against tightly coupled service discovery libraries; I will discuss that in more depth in the next section of the chapter.

To run the service in Docker, use the following `docker run` command:

```
$ docker run -p 5001:5001 -e PORT=5001 \
    -e EUREKA__CLIENT__SERVICEURL=http://192.168.0.33:8080/eureka/ \
    dotnetcoreservices/ecommerce-inventory
```

When you provide the configuration overrides here, make sure you use your actual machine's IP address. When running inside the Docker image, referring to `localhost` doesn't do anyone any good.

And finally, start the catalog service on port 5001:

```
$ cd <catalog service>
$ dotnet run --server.urls=http://0.0.0.0:5002
```

Now you can issue the appropriate GET requests to the product API for the product list and product details:

GET `http://localhost:5002/api/products`
> Retrieve product list

GET `http://localhost:5002/api/products/{id}`
> Retrieve product details, which will invoke the inventory service, whose URL is dynamically discovered via Eureka

DNS and Platform Supported Discovery

This chapter has basically showed you that through the use of an open source server product and a few client libraries, you can write code to consume URLs in the format `http://service/api` and assume that the library code will swap the word *service* for a fully qualified domain name or an IP address.

The main problem I have with this pattern is that it has the side effect of tightly coupling application code with a particular server and client implementation of service discovery. For example, using Eureka (including the helper classes that come with Steeltoe), there's still code that has to manually replace logical service descriptors (e.g., `inventory`) with IP addresses or fully qualified domain names like `inventory.mycluster.mycorp.com`.

Service discovery, registration, and fault detection are all things that I feel should be *nonfunctional requirements*. As such, application code shouldn't contain anything that tightly couples it to some implementation of service discovery.

Obviously, reality and pragmatism must prevail and the decision is ultimately yours, but there are ways to do service discovery without incurring some of the baggage you might get from diving into the deep end with Netflix OSS and Eureka.

Platforms like Kubernetes have plug-ins like SkyDNS (*https://github.com/skynetservices/skydns*) that will automatically synchronize information about deployed and running services with a network-local DNS table. This means that without *any* client or server dependencies, you can simply consume a service at a URL like `http://inventory` and your client code will automatically resolve to an appropriate IP address.

When evaluating how you're going to do discovery, you should see if there might be a way to accomplish it without creating a tight coupling or dependency in your application code.

Summary

If you're building microservices today, then you're likely not building just one that runs in isolation. Figuring out a reliable way of allowing one service to be aware of the URLs and status of all the services on which it depends is no small task. If the idea of dynamic runtime service discovery and of using such discovery to support failover and fault tolerance appeals to you, then a registry like Eureka might be for you.

Keep in mind, though, that a dynamic service registry like Eureka is just one tool among many in the vast arsenal at our disposal these days for building service ecosystems. Hopefully this chapter will have given you an idea of some of the possibilities available and provided enough details for you to decide whether you're going to use discovery with your project.

CHAPTER 9

Configuring Microservice Ecosystems

Configuration is one of the areas of architecture and implementation that are often overlooked by product teams. A lot of teams just assume that the legacy paradigms for configuring applications will work fine in the cloud. Further, it's easy to assume that you'll "just" inject all configuration through environment variables.

Configuration in a microservice ecosystem requires attention to a number of other factors, including:

- Securing read and write access to configuration values
- Ensuring that an audit trail of value changes is available
- Resilience and reliability of the source of configuration information
- Support for large and complex configuration information likely too burdensome to cram into a handful of environment variables
- Determining whether your application needs to respond to live updates or real-time changes in configuration values, and if so, how to provision for that
- Ability to support things like feature flags and complex hierarchies of settings
- Possibly supporting the storage and retrieval of secure (encrypted) information or the encryption keys themselves

Not every team has to worry about all of these things, but this is just a hint as to the complexity of configuration management lying below the surface waiting to strike those who underestimate this problem.

This chapter will begin by talking about the mechanics of using environment variables in an application and illustrate Docker's support for this. Next, we'll explore a configuration server product from the Netflix OSS stack. Finally, we'll dive deeper into etcd, an open source distributed key-value store often used for configuration management.

Using Environment Variables with Docker

It is actually fairly easy to work with environment variables and Docker. This book has harped on this point a number of times. Cloud-native applications need to be able to accept configuration through environment variables. While you might accept more robust configuration mechanisms (we'll discuss those shortly), environment variables supplied by the *platform* on which you deploy should the minimal level of configuration support your applications have.

Even if you have a default set of configuration available, you should figure out which settings can be overridden by environment variables at application startup.

You can explicitly set configuration values using name-value pairs as shown in the following command:

```
$ sudo docker run -e SOME_VAR='foo' \
  -e PASSWORD='foo' \
  -e USER='bar' \
  -e DB_NAME='mydb' \
  -p 3000:3000 \
  --name container_name microservices-aspnetcore/image:tag
```

Or, if you want to avoid passing explicit values on the command line, you can *forward* environment variables from the launching environment into the container by simply not passing values or using the equals sign, as shown here:

```
$ docker run -e PORT -e CLIENTSECRET -e CLIENTKEY [...]
```

This will take the PORT, CLIENTSECRET, and CLIENTKEY environment variables from the shell in which the command was run and pass their values into the Docker container without exposing their values on the command line, preventing a potential security vulnerability or leaking of confidential information.

If you have a large number of environment variables to pass into your container, you can give the docker command the name of a file that contains name-value pairs:

```
$ docker run --env-file ./myenv.file [...]
```

If you're running a higher-level container orchestration tool like Kubernetes, then you will have access to more elegant ways to manage your environment variables and how they get injected into your containers. With Kubernetes, you can use a concept called ConfigMap to make external configuration values available to your containers without having to create complex launch commands or manage bloated start scripts.

A deep dive into container orchestration systems is beyond the scope of this book, but this should reinforce the idea that no matter what your ultimate deployment target is going to be, *all* of them should have some means of injecting environment variables so your application *must* know how to accept those values.

By supporting environment variable injection and sticking with Docker as your unit of immutable artifact deployment, you're well positioned to run in any number of environments without becoming too tightly coupled to any one in particular.

Using Spring Cloud Config Server

One of the biggest difficulties surrounding configuration management for services lies not in the mechanics of injecting values into environment variables, but in the day-to-day maintenance of the values themselves.

How do we know when the ultimate source of truth for the configuration values has changed? How do we know *who* changed them, and how do we implement security controls to prevent these values from being changed by unauthorized personnel and keep the values hidden from those without appropriate access?

Further, if values do change, how do we go back and see what the previous values were? If you're thinking that we could use a solution like a Git repository to manage configuration values, then you're not alone.

The folks who built Spring Cloud Config Server (SCCS) had the same idea. Why reinvent the wheel (security, version control, auditing, etc.) when Git has already solved the problem? Instead they built a service that exposes the values contained in a Git repository through a RESTful API.

This API exposes URLs in the following format:

```
/{application}/{profile}[/{label}]
/{application}-{profile}.yml
/{label}/{application}-{profile}.yml
/{application}-{profile}.properties
/{label}/{application}-{profile}.properties
```

If your application is named foo, then all of the {application} segments in the preceding template would be replaced with foo. To see the configuration values available in the development profile (environment), you would issue a GET request to the /foo/development URL.

To find out more about Spring Cloud Config Server, you can start with the documentation (*http://bit.ly/2wkeZNF*).

While the documentation and code are targeted at Java developers, there are plenty of other clients that can talk to SCCS, including a .NET Core client that is part of the Steeltoe project (discussed in the previous chapter).

To add client-side support for SCCS to our .NET Core application, we just need to add a reference to the Steeltoe.Extensions.Configuration.ConfigServer NuGet package.

Next, we need to configure our application so it can get the right settings from the right place. This means we need to define a Spring application name and give the URL to the configuration server in our *appsettings.json* file (remember every setting in this file can be overridden with environment variables):

```
{
  "spring": {
    "application": {
      "name": "foo"
    },
    "cloud": {
      "config": {
        "uri": "http://localhost:8888"
      }
    }
  },
  "Logging": {
    "IncludeScopes": false,
    "LogLevel": {
      "Default": "Debug",
      "System": "Information",
      "Microsoft": "Information"
    }
  }
}
```

With this configuration set up, our `Startup` method looks almost exactly like it does in most of our other applications:

```
public Startup(IHostingEnvironment env)
{
    var builder = new ConfigurationBuilder()
        .SetBasePath(env.ContentRootPath)
        .AddJsonFile("appsettings.json", optional: false,
            reloadOnChange: false)
        .AddEnvironmentVariables()
        .AddConfigServer(env);

    Configuration = builder.Build();
}
```

The next changes required to add support for the configuration server come in the `ConfigureServices` method. First, we call `AddConfigServer`, which enables the client through dependency injection. Next, we call `Configure` with a generic type parameter. This allows us to capture the application's settings as retrieved from the server in an `IOptionsSnapshot`, which is then available for injection into our controllers and other code:

```
public void ConfigureServices(IServiceCollection services)
{
    services.AddConfigServer(Configuration);
```

```
        services.AddMvc();

        services.Configure<ConfigServerData>(Configuration);
    }
```

The class we're using here to hold the data from the config server is modeled after the sample configuration that can be found in the Spring Cloud server sample repository (*https://github.com/spring-cloud-samples/config-repo*):

```
public class ConfigServerData
{
    public string Bar { get; set; }
    public string Foo { get; set; }
    public Info Info { get; set; }

}

public class Info
{
    public string Description { get; set; }
    public string Url { get; set; }
}
```

We can then inject our C# class as well as the configuration server client settings if we need them:

```
public class MyController : Controller
{
    private IOptionsSnapshot<ConfigServerData>
      MyConfiguration { get; set; }

    private ConfigServerClientSettingsOptions
      ConfigServerClientSettingsOptions { get; set; }

    public MyController(IOptionsSnapShot<ConfigServerData> opts,
                        IOptions<ConfigServerClientSettingsOptions>
                            clientOpts)
    {
        ...
    }

      ....
}
```

With this setup in place, and a running configuration server, the opts variable in the constructor will contain all of the relevant configuration for our application.

To run the config server, we can build and launch the code from GitHub if we want, but not all of us have a functioning Java/Maven development environment up and running (and some of us simply don't *want* a Java environment). The easiest way to start a configuration server is to just launch it from a Docker image:

```
$ docker run -p 8888:8888 \
  -e SPRING_CLOUD_CONFIG_SERVER_GIT_URI=https://github.com/spring-cloud-samples/ \
  config-repohyness/spring-cloud-config-server
```

This will start the server and point it at the sample GitHub repo mentioned earlier to obtain the "foo" application's configuration properties. If the server is running properly, you should get some meaningful information from the following command:

```
$ curl http://localhost:8888/foo/development
```

With a config server Docker image running locally and the C# code illustrated in this section of the chapter, you should be able to play with exposing external configuration data to your .NET Core microservices.

Before continuing on to the next chapter, you should experiment with the Steeltoe configuration server client sample (*http://bit.ly/2u0WUzF*) and then take stock of the options available to you for externalizing configuration.

Configuring Microservices with etcd

Not everyone wants to use the Netflix OSS stack, for a number of reasons. For one, it is noticeably Java-heavy—all of the advanced development in that stack occurs in Java first, and all of the other clients (including C#) are delayed ports of the original. Some developers are fine with this; others may not like it.

Others may also take umbrage with the size of the Spring Cloud Config Server. It is a Spring boot application but it consumes a pretty hefty chunk of memory, and if you're running multiple instances of it to ensure resilience and to prevent any of your applications from failing to obtain configuration, you could end up consuming a lot of the underlying virtual resources just to support configuration.

There is no end to the number of alternatives to Spring Cloud Config Server, but one very popular alternative is etcd. As mentioned briefly in the previous chapter, etcd is a lightweight, distributed key-value store.

This is where you put the most critical information required to support a distributed system. etcd is a clustered product that uses the Raft (*https://raft.github.io/*) consensus algorithm to communicate with peers. There are more than 500 projects on GitHub that rely on etcd. One of the most common use cases for etcd is the storage and retrieval of configuration information and feature flags.

To get started with etcd, check out the documentation (*https://coreos.com/etcd/*). You can install a local version of it (it really is a small-footprint server) or you can run it from a Docker image.

Another option is to use a cloud-hosted version. For the sample in this chapter, I went over to compose.io and signed up for a free trial hosting of etcd (you *will* have to supply a credit card, but they won't charge you if you cancel within the trial period).

To work with the key-value hierarchy in etcd that resembles a simple folder structure, you're going to need the etcdctl command-line utility. This comes for free when you install etcd. On a Mac, you can just brew install etcd and you'll have access to the tool. Check the documentation for Windows and Linux instructions.

The etcdctl command requires you to pass the addresses of the cluster peers as well as the username and password and other options *every time* you run it. To make this far less annoying, I created an alias as follows:

```
$ alias e='etcdctl --no-sync \
    --peers https://portal1934-21.euphoric-etcd-31.host.host.composedb.com:17174,\
    https://portal2016-22.euphoric-etcd-31.host.host.composedb.com:17174 \
    -u root:password'
```

You'll want to change *root:password* to something that actually applies to your installation, regardless of whether you're running locally or cloud-hosted.

Now that you've got the alias configured and you have access to a running copy of etcd, you can issue some basic commands:

mk
Creates a key and can optionally create directories if you define a deep path for the key.

set
Sets a key's value.

rm
Removes a key.

ls
Queries for a list of subkeys below the parent. In keeping with the filesystem analogy, this works like listing the files in a directory.

update
Updates a key value.

watch
Watches a key for changes to its value.

Armed with a command-line utility, let's issue a few commands:

```
$ e ls /
$ e set myapp/hello world
world
$ e set myapp/rate 12.5
12.5
```

```
$ e ls
/myapp
$ e ls /myapp
/myapp/hello
/myapp/rate
$ e get /myapp/rate
12.5
```

This session first examined the root and saw that there was nothing there. Then, the myapp/hello key was created with the value world and the myapp/rate key was created with the value 12.5. This implicitly created */myapp* as a parent key/directory. Because of its status as a parent, it didn't have a value.

After running these commands, I refreshed my fancy dashboard on compose.io's website and saw the newly created keys and their values, as shown in Figure 9-1.

Figure 9-1. Compose.io's etcd dashboard

This is great—we have a configuration server and it has data ready for us to consume —but how are we going to consume it? To do that we're going to create a custom ASP.NET configuration provider.

Creating an etcd Configuration Provider

Throughout the book we've gone through a number of different ways to consume the ASP.NET configuration system. You've seen to how add multiple different configuration sources with the AddJsonFile and AddEnvironmentVariables methods.

Our goal now is to add an AddEtcdConfiguration method that plugs into a running etcd server and grabs values that appear as though they are a native part of the ASP.NET configuration system.

Creating a configuration source

The first thing we need to do is add a configuration source. The job of a configuration source is to create an instance of a configuration builder. Thankfully these are pretty simple interfaces and there's already a starter `ConfigurationBuilder` class for us to build upon.

Here's the new configuration source:

```
using System;
using Microsoft.Extensions.Configuration;

namespace ConfigClient
{
    public class EtcdConfigurationSource : IConfigurationSource
    {
        public EtcdConnectionOptions Options { get; set; }

        public EtcdConfigurationSource(
          EtcdConnectionOptions options)
        {
            this.Options = options;
        }

        public IConfigurationProvider Build(
          IConfigurationBuilder builder)
        {
            return new EtcdConfigurationProvider(this);
        }
    }
}
```

There is some basic amount of information that we'll need in order to communicate with `etcd`. You'll recognize this information as mostly the same values we supplied to the CLI earlier:

```
public class EtcdConnectionOptions
{
    public string[] Urls { get; set; }
    public string Username { get; set; }
    public string Password { get; set; }
    public string RootKey { get; set; }
}
```

Creating a configuration builder

Next we can create a configuration builder. The base class from which we'll inherit maintains a protected dictionary called `Data` that stores simple key-value pairs. This is convenient for a sample, so we'll use that now. More advanced configuration providers for `etcd` would probably want the flexibility of maybe splitting keys on the / character and building a hierarchy of configuration sections, so `/myapp/rate` would become `myapp:rate` (nested sections) rather than a single section named `/myapp/rate`:

```csharp
using System;
using System.Collections.Generic;
using EtcdNet;
using Microsoft.Extensions.Configuration;
using Microsoft.Extensions.Primitives;

namespace ConfigClient
{
    public class EtcdConfigurationProvider : ConfigurationProvider
    {
        private EtcdConfigurationSource source;

        public EtcdConfigurationProvider(
          EtcdConfigurationSource source)
        {
            this.source = source;
        }

        public override void Load()
        {
            EtcdClientOpitions options = new EtcdClientOpitions()
            {
                Urls = source.Options.Urls,
                Username = source.Options.Username,
                Password = source.Options.Password,
                UseProxy = false,
                IgnoreCertificateError = true
            };
            EtcdClient etcdClient = new EtcdClient(options);
            try
            {
                EtcdResponse resp =
                 etcdClient.GetNodeAsync(source.Options.RootKey,
                    recursive: true, sorted: true).Result;
                if (resp.Node.Nodes != null)
                {
                    foreach (var node in resp.Node.Nodes)
                    {
                        // child node
                        Data[node.Key] = node.Value;
                    }
                }
            }
            catch (EtcdCommonException.KeyNotFound)
            {
                // key does not
                Console.WriteLine("key not found exception");
            }
        }
    }
}
```

The important part of this code is highlighted in bold. It calls GetNodeAsync and then iterates over a *single* level of child nodes. A production-grade library might recursively sift through an entire tree until it had fetched all values. Each key-value pair retrieved from etcd is simply added to the protected Data member.

This code uses an open source module available on NuGet called EtcdNet. At the time I wrote this book, this was the most stable and reliable of the few I could find that were compatible with .NET Core.

With a simple extension method like this:

```
public static class EtcdStaticExtensions
{
    public static IConfigurationBuilder AddEtcdConfiguration(
        this IConfigurationBuilder builder,
        EtcdConnectionOptions connectionOptions)
    {
        return builder.Add(
          new EtcdConfigurationSource(connectionOptions));
    }
}
```

We can add etcd as a configuration source in our Startup class:

```
public Startup(IHostingEnvironment env)
{
    var builder = new ConfigurationBuilder()
        .SetBasePath(env.ContentRootPath)
        .AddJsonFile("appsettings.json", optional: false, reloadOnChange: true)
        .AddEtcdConfiguration(new EtcdConnectionOptions
        {
            Urls = new string[] {
            "https://(host1):17174",
            "https://(host2):17174"
             },
            Username = "root",
            Password = "(hidden)",
            RootKey = "/myapp"
        })
        .AddEnvironmentVariables();
    Configuration = builder.Build();
}
```

For obvious reasons, I've snipped out the root password for the instance. Yours will vary depending on how you installed etcd or where you're hosting it. If you end up going this route, you'll probably want to "bootstrap" the connection information to the config server with environment variables containing the peer URLs, the username, and the password.

Using the etcd configuration values

There's just one last thing to do, and that's make sure that our application is aware of the values we're getting from the configuration source. To do that, we can add a somewhat dirty hack to the "values" controller you get from the webapi scaffolding:

```
using System;
using System.Collections.Generic;
using System.Linq;
using System.Threading.Tasks;
using Microsoft.AspNetCore.Mvc;
using EtcdNet;
using Microsoft.Extensions.Logging;
using Microsoft.Extensions.Configuration;

namespace ConfigClient.Controllers
{
    [Route("api/[controller]")]
    public class ValuesController : Controller
    {
        private ILogger logger;

        public ValuesController(ILogger<ValuesController> logger)
        {
            this.logger = logger;
        }

        // GET api/values
        [HttpGet]
        public IEnumerable<string> Get()
        {
            List<string> values = new List<string>();
            values.Add(
              Startup.Configuration.GetSection("/myapp/hello").Value);
            values.Add(
              Startup.Configuration.GetSection("/myapp/rate").Value);

            return values;
        }

    // ... snip ...
    }
}
```

To keep the code listing down I snipped out the rest of the boilerplate from the values controller. With a reference to EtcdNet in the project's *.csproj* file, you can dotnet restore and then dotnet run the application.

Hitting the http://localhost:3000/api/values endpoint now returns these values:

```
["world","12.5"]
```

These are the exact values that we added to our etcd server earlier in the section. With just a handful of lines of code we were able to add a rock-solid, remote configuration server as a standards-conforming ASP.NET configuration source!

Summary

There are a million different ways to solve the problem of configuring microservices, and this chapter only showed you a small sample of these. While you're free to chose whichever you like, keep a close eye on how you're going to maintain your configuration *after* your application is up and running in production. Do you need audit controls, security, revision history, and other Git-like features?

Your platform might come with its own way of helping you inject and manage configuration, but the single most important lesson to learn from this chapter is that every single application and service you build *must* be able to accept external configuration through environment variables, and anything more complicated than a handful of environment variables is likely going to require some kind of external, out-of-process configuration management service.

CHAPTER 10

Securing Applications and Microservices

Developers' perception of security concerns can range from true love to pure evil. In some organizations, security is a checklist that happens after an application has been developed, and in others it is such a burden that it often doesn't get done properly or is simply skipped altogether.

When building applications for the cloud—applications built around the assumption that they might not run on infrastructure you own—security *cannot* be an afterthought or some mindless checkbox on a to-do list. Security must be a first-class citizen in all development efforts for user-facing applications and services alike.

In this chapter we'll discuss security topics as they relate to cloud-native applications and develop samples that illustrate some ways we can secure our ASP.NET Core web applications and microservices.

Security in the Cloud

Securing applications that run at scale in the cloud is not as straightforward as it is when you deploy applications to a local data center where you have full control over the operating system and the installation environment.

In this section, we'll cover some of the main issues that developers often run into when trying to adapt their existing ASP.NET skills or legacy codebases to running securely in the cloud. Some of these problems might be obvious (like the lack of Windows authentication), whereas others are more subtle.

Intranet Applications

Intranet applications are everywhere and are often as complex (or more so!) than customer-facing applications. Companies build these support or line-of-business applications all the time, but when we think about building such applications running on a PaaS on top of scalable, cloud infrastructure, some of our old patterns and practices fall short.

The most notable issue is the inability to do *Windows authentication*. ASP.NET developers have been spoiled by a long history of built-in support for securing web applications with Windows credentials. In these applications, the browser-based challenge replies with details about the currently logged-in user, and the server knows how to deal with that information and the user is implicitly logged in. This is extremely effective and very handy for building apps secured against a company's internal Active Directory.

The reason this works is because the client browser and the server application are part of the same domain, or workgroup, or interoperable domains. The presence of Windows on the server and client as well as the presence of Kerberos in the middle facilitate this seamless exchange of credentials.

Whether you're running in a public cloud or your own on-premise PaaS, these platforms operate very differently from traditional physical or virtual machine Windows deployments.

The operating system that underpins your application needs to be considered *ephemeral*. It is subject to periodic and random destruction. You cannot assume that it will have the ability to join a domain; in fact, it is highly unlikely that domain joining will be a practical option. In a lot of cases, the operating systems supporting your cloud applications are frequently and deliberately destroyed. Some companies have security policies where all virtual machines are destroyed and rebuilt during rolling updates to reduce the potential surface area exposed for persistent attacks.

In the case of the code we're writing for this book, we're restricting ourselves to the cross-platform variant of .NET Core, so we can't rely on any facilities that are only available to Windows applications. This rules out integrated Windows authentication, so we'll need to find a different alternative for our cloud services.

Cookie and Forms Authentication

Anyone who has worked with legacy ASP.NET web applications should be familiar with forms authentication. This mode of authentication is where an application presents a custom UI (a form) to prompt the users for their credentials. The credentials are transmitted directly to the application and validated by the application.

When users successfully log in, they receive a cookie that marks them as authenticated for some period of time.

There is nothing about running your application on PaaS that is intrinsically good or bad for cookie authentication. However, it does create a few additional burdens for your application.

First and foremost, forms authentication requires your application to maintain and validate credentials. This means you'll have to deal with securing, encrypting, and storing confidential information. As we'll see later in the chapter, there are other options available that let us defer the maintenance and validation of identity to third parties, allowing our apps to focus solely on their core business value.

Encryption for Apps in the Cloud

Encryption is usually something that we worry about on a per-application basis. Some services use encryption and others don't. In the days of legacy ASP.NET applications, we would find the most common use of encryption in the creation of secure authentication and session cookies.

This form of encryption would make use of the *machine key* in order to encrypt cookies. It would then use the same machine key to decrypt cookies sent to the web application from the browser.

The simple phrase "machine key" should scare us to death as developers of cloud-native services. In the cloud, we can't rely on specific machines or on specific files sitting on those machines. Our application can start up inside any container at any time, hosted by any number of virtual machines on any number of continents. We simply cannot rely on the fact that a single encryption key will be distributed across every machine on which our application runs.

As we'll discuss throughout the rest of the chapter, there are a number of other areas where encryption is used. For example, tokens are often cryptographically signed, requiring the use of asymmetric keys for validation.

Where do you store your keys if you cannot rely on the existence of a persistent filesystem, nor can you rely on those keys being available in the memory of every running instance of your service?

The answer is to treat the storage and maintenance of cryptographic keys as a backing service. In other words, this service is external to your application, in the same way that state, the filesystem, databases, and additional microservices are.

Bearer Tokens

If an application isn't the central authority on the identity and authorization of its users, then it needs to be coded in such a way that it can accept *proof of identity* and *proof of authorization.* There are a number of different standards that define various methods for accepting proof of identity, including OAuth and OpenID Connect (usually just referred to as OIDC) that we'll be illustrating in this chapter's samples.

The most common way to transmit proof of identity in an HTTP-friendly, portable manner is through the use of *bearer tokens*. Ideally, when an application accepts a bearer token it does so through the Authorization header. The following shows an example of what a bearer token might look like in an HTTP trace:

```
POST /api/service HTTP/1.1
Host: world-domination.io
Authorization: Bearer ABC123HIJABC123HIJABC123HIJ
Content-Type: application/x-www-form-urlencoded
User-Agent: Mozilla/5.0 (X11; Linux x86_64) etc...etc...etc...
```

The value of the Authorization header takes the form of a single word that indicates the type of authorization, followed by some sequence of characters that contains the value of the credentials. You might be more familiar with other commonly used authorization types: Digest and Basic.

In a normal service flow that utilizes bearer tokens, the service will extract the token from the Authorization header. Many token formats, like OAuth 2.0 (JWT), are usually encoded in a Base64, URL-friendly format, so the first step toward validating those tokens is decoding them to get at the original content. If a token was encrypted with a private key, a service will then use a public key to validate that the token was produced by the appropriate authority.

For a detailed discussion of the JSON Web Token (JWT) format and specifications, feel free to check out the original RFC (*https://tools.ietf.org/html/rfc7519*). The code samples we're going to be looking at in this chapter will make extensive use of the JWT format.

Securing ASP.NET Core Web Apps

Securing an ASP.NET Core web application involves deciding on authentication and authorization mechanisms and then using the appropriate middleware. Authentication middleware examines incoming HTTP requests, determines if the user is authenticated, and, if not, issues the appropriate challenge and redirects.

One of the most reliable ways to perform authentication in the cloud and keep your applications as focused on business logic as possible is through the use of bearer tokens.

For the samples in this chapter, we'll be focusing on OpenID Connect and bearer tokens using the JWT standard.

OpenID Connect Primer

Depending on the type of application we're building and the security requirements of that application, we have a wide variety of authentication flows that we can utilize. OpenID Connect (we'll just refer to it as OIDC from now on) is a superset of the OAuth2 standard and contains specifications and standards for the ways identity providers (IDPs), users, and applications communicate securely.

There are authorization flows that are designed specifically for single-page web applications, for mobile applications, and for traditional web applications. One of the simpler flows available for web applications is the one shown in the sequence diagram in Figure 10-1.

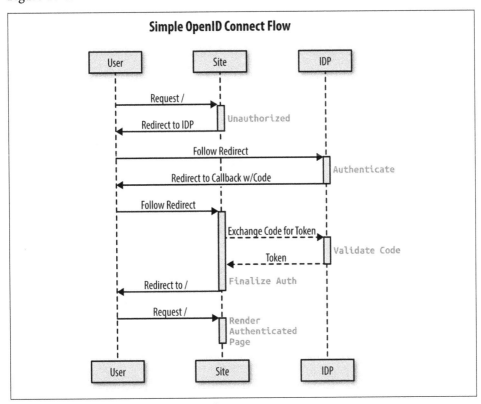

Figure 10-1. Simple OpenID Connect flow

In this flow, an unauthenticated user makes a request for a protected resource on a website. The site then redirects the user to the identity provider, giving it instructions on how to call the site back after authentication. If all goes well, the identity provider will supply to the site a short string with a very short expiration period called a *code*. The site (also referred to as the *protected resource* in this scenario) will then immediately make an HTTP POST call to the identity provider that includes a client ID, a client secret, and the code. In return, the IDP gives back an OIDC token (in JWT format).

Once the site has received and validated the token, it knows that the user is properly authenticated. The site can then write an authentication cookie and redirect to a home page or the original protected resource. The presence of the cookie is now used so the site can bypass the round-trip to the IDP.

There are more complex flows that include the concept of resources and obtaining access tokens with more chatty redirect loops, but for our sample we're going to be using the simplest flow. This flow is also one of the more secure because the claims-bearing token is never exposed on a URL, only as a short-lived string that is immediately swapped over a secure connection for a token.

OIDC References and Resources

For a more thorough examination of OpenID Connect, its history beginning with the original OAuth standard, and many other security and authentication concepts, I recommend you check out the book *Identity & Data Security for Web Development* by Jonathan LeBlanc and Tim Messerschmidt (O'Reilly). The code samples are in Node.js, but they're easy enough to read and the book is worth the read for the explanations of authentication standards alone.

It might seem a little complex now, but as you get more exposure to OIDC and you see how little code you have to implement (thanks to readily available open source middleware), it becomes less intimidating.

Securing an ASP.NET Core App with OIDC

For our first code sample in this chapter, we're going to take a simple ASP.NET Core MVC web application and secure it with OIDC. To do this, we're going to need a few things:

- An empty web application
- An identity provider
- Some OIDC middleware

Creating an empty web application

The first of the three is easily taken care of with the following command at a terminal:

```
$ dotnet new mvc
```

This creates a starter web application using MVC with a stock controller and some basic layouts, CSS, and JavaScript. We're going to use this as a starting point to add security. If you want to see the completed code sample, you can find it on GitHub (*http://bit.ly/2hqSa4w*).

Setting up an identity provider with an Auth0 account

Now that we have an unsecured application, we need to figure out what we're going to use as our identity provider. In an enterprise situation, we might use something like Active Directory Federation Services (ADFS). If we're already invested in Azure and running an Active Directory there, we might secure our application with Azure AD. We could also use other IDPs, like Ping Federate or Forge Rock. There are plenty of open source samples for standing up super-simple IDPs for experimentation and testing, too.

For the purposes of giving you a sample that you can use without investing in a pile of infrastructure or shelling out a bunch of money in upfront costs, we want an easy-to-use identity provider that includes a free trial period. I decided on Auth0 for this chapter, but other providers are available, like Google and Stormpath (which is merging with Okta (*https://stormpath.com/blog/stormpaths-new-path*)). Using Google as an IDP will only accept Google identities, whereas Auth0, Stormpath, and their ilk can be configured to use a private database of users or accept other common OIDC identities, like Facebook and Twitter.

Take a moment now to go over to *http://auth0.com*. Once you've signed up and are at your dashboard, click the Create Client button. Make sure you choose Regular Web Application as the application type. If you choose ASP.NET Core as the implementation language, you will be taken to a quick-start tutorial with code that looks very similar to what we're going to build in this chapter.

Configuring Your Auth0 Client

It is important that you follow all of the directions at the beginning of the Auth0 .NET Core tutorial. This means changing the OAuth JWT signature algorithm under Advanced Settings to RS256.

For the sample client used in this chapter I created a connection to a private database of users, but you can choose what you like, including accepting identities from Facebook or Twitter.

Using the OIDC middleware

Thankfully we have been spared the burden of having to write all of the code that implements the redirects and the other low-level details of the OIDC standard. All we have to do is decide when we want to initiate a challenge (force a user to authenticate against the IDP) and configure the OIDC middleware.

Take a look at the modified *Startup.cs* file from our previously empty web application, shown in Example 10-1. We'll analyze what's going on next.

Example 10-1. src/StatlerWaldorfCorp.SecureWebApp/Startup.cs

```
using System;
using System.Collections.Generic;
using System.Linq;
using System.Security.Claims;
using System.Threading.Tasks;
using Microsoft.AspNetCore.Builder;
using Microsoft.AspNetCore.Hosting;
using Microsoft.Extensions.Configuration;
using Microsoft.Extensions.DependencyInjection;
using Microsoft.Extensions.Logging;
using Microsoft.Extensions.Options;
using Microsoft.AspNetCore.Authentication.Cookies;
using Microsoft.AspNetCore.Authentication.OpenIdConnect;
using Microsoft.AspNetCore.Http;


namespace StatlerWaldorfCorp.SecureWebApp
{
    public class Startup
    {
        public Startup(IHostingEnvironment env)
        {
            var builder = new ConfigurationBuilder()
                .SetBasePath(env.ContentRootPath)
                .AddJsonFile("appsettings.json",
                  optional: true, reloadOnChange: false)
                .AddEnvironmentVariables();
            Configuration = builder.Build();
        }

        public IConfigurationRoot Configuration { get; }

        public void ConfigureServices(IServiceCollection services)
        {
            services.AddAuthentication(
                options => options.SignInScheme =
              CookieAuthenticationDefaults.AuthenticationScheme);
```

```
    // Add framework services.
    services.AddMvc();

    services.AddOptions();

    services.Configure<OpenIDSettings>(
      Configuration.GetSection("OpenID"));
}

public void Configure(IApplicationBuilder app,
            IHostingEnvironment env,
            ILoggerFactory loggerFactory,
            IOptions<OpenIDSettings> openIdSettings)
{
    Console.WriteLine("Using OpenID Auth domain of : " +
      openIdSettings.Value.Domain);
    loggerFactory.AddConsole(
      Configuration.GetSection("Logging"));
    loggerFactory.AddDebug();

    if (env.IsDevelopment())
    {
        app.UseDeveloperExceptionPage();
    }
    else
    {
        app.UseExceptionHandler("/Home/Error");
    }

    app.UseStaticFiles();

    app.UseCookieAuthentication(
      new CookieAuthenticationOptions
      {
          AutomaticAuthenticate = true,
          AutomaticChallenge = true
      });

    var options =
      CreateOpenIdConnectOptions(openIdSettings);
    options.Scope.Clear();
    options.Scope.Add("openid");
    options.Scope.Add("name");
    options.Scope.Add("email");
    options.Scope.Add("picture");

    app.UseOpenIdConnectAuthentication(options);

    app.UseMvc(routes =>
    {
        routes.MapRoute(
            name: "default",
```

```
                    template: "{controller=Home}/{action=Index}/{id?}");
        });
    }

    private OpenIdConnectOptions CreateOpenIdConnectOptions(
        IOptions<OpenIDSettings> openIdSettings)
    {
        return new OpenIdConnectOptions("Auth0")
        {
            Authority =
              $"https://{openIdSettings.Value.Domain}",
            ClientId = openIdSettings.Value.ClientId,
            ClientSecret = openIdSettings.Value.ClientSecret,
            AutomaticAuthenticate = false,
            AutomaticChallenge = false,

            ResponseType = "code",
            CallbackPath = new PathString("/signin-auth0"),

            ClaimsIssuer = "Auth0",
            SaveTokens = true,
            Events = CreateOpenIdConnectEvents()
        };
    }

    private OpenIdConnectEvents CreateOpenIdConnectEvents()
    {
        return new OpenIdConnectEvents()
        {
            OnTicketReceived = context =>
            {
              var identity =
                context.Principal.Identity as ClaimsIdentity;
              if (identity != null) {
                if (!context.Principal.HasClaim(
                    c => c.Type == ClaimTypes.Name) &&
                    identity.HasClaim( c => c.Type == "name"))
                      identity.AddClaim(
                          new Claim(ClaimTypes.Name,
                              identity.FindFirst("name").Value));
              }
              return Task.FromResult(0);
            }
        };
    }
  }
}
```

The first thing that looks different from the samples in previous chapters is that we're
making an options class called OpenIDSettings available as a service by reading it

from the configuration system. This is a plain class that just exposes properties for holding the four pieces of metadata needed for every OIDC client:

Authorization domain
> The root hostname of the IDP.

Client ID
> An ID issued by the IDP. You can see this on your client configuration page in Auth0.

Client secret
> There is a button on your Auth0 client configuration page to copy this value to the clipboard.

Callback URL
> This tells the IDP how to redirect the user back to your site after authentication. This value must be configured in the list of authorized callback URLs in your Auth0 client configuration.

Because of the sensitive nature of this information, we haven't checked our *appsettings.json* file into GitHub, but Example 10-2 shows what it looks like.

Example 10-2. appsettings.json

```
{
  "Logging": {
    "IncludeScopes": false,
    "LogLevel": {
      "Default": "Debug",
      "System": "Information",
      "Microsoft": "Information"
    }
  },
  "OpenID": {
      "Domain" : "bestbookeverwritten.auth0.com",
      "ClientId" : "<client id>",
      "ClientSecret": "<client secret>",
      "CallbackUrl": "http://localhost:5000/signin-auth0"
  }
}
```

The next two things we do in our new startup class are tell ASP.NET Core that we want cookie authentication and that we want OpenID Connect authentication. Remember that we use OIDC to *determine* who the users are and if they're authenticated, and we'll use cookies to *remember* who they are until the cookies expire.

Another key piece of code is in the `CreateOpenIdConnectEvents` method. Here we define a function that is invoked after we get an authentication ticket back from the

IDP. We use this to sift through the claims on the ticket, and if we find a name claim, we add it to the current claims identity using a well-known constant for the appropriate claim type. This has the effect of translating the OIDC token name claim into the Name property on the ClaimsIdentity. Without this bit of code, we would appear to authenticate but the user's name would be null.

Microsoft Claims Versus OpenID Claims

The issue at hand is that the identity system for ASP.NET Core relies on the ClaimTypes.Name constant (http://sche mas.xmlsoap.org/ws/2005/05/identity/claims/name) to determine the name of the user. However, the name of the claim that corresponds to user name on an OpenID JWT token is simply name. Any time we merge OIDC identity and ASP.NET identity, we have to translate claims like this.

If we were to run the application right now, it would appear as though we've done nothing. The application still accepts anonymous authentication and there's nothing that triggers an authentication flow with the Auth0 IDP.

To facilitate this new functionality, we're going to add an account controller as shown in Example 10-3. This controller exposes actions for logging in, logging out, and rendering a view that displays all of the claims on the user identity.

Example 10-3. src/StatlerWaldorfCorp.SecureWebApp.Controllers.AccountController

```
using Microsoft.AspNetCore.Authentication.Cookies;
using Microsoft.AspNetCore.Mvc;
using Microsoft.AspNetCore.Http.Authentication;
using Microsoft.AspNetCore.Authorization;
using System.Linq;
using System.Security.Claims;

namespace StatlerWaldorfCorp.SecureWebApp.Controllers
{
    public class AccountController : Controller
    {
        public IActionResult Login(string returnUrl = "/")
        {
            return new ChallengeResult("Auth0",
            new AuthenticationProperties() {
              RedirectUri = returnUrl
            });
        }

        [Authorize]
        public IActionResult Logout()
        {
```

```
        HttpContext.Authentication.SignOutAsync("Auth0");
        HttpContext.Authentication.SignOutAsync(
          CookieAuthenticationDefaults.AuthenticationScheme);

        return RedirectToAction("Index", "Home");
    }

    [Authorize]
    public IActionResult Claims()
    {
        ViewData["Title"] = "Claims";
        var identity =
          HttpContext.User.Identity as ClaimsIdentity;
        ViewData["picture"] =
          identity.FindFirst("picture").Value;
        return View();
    }
  }
}
```

Take a look at the code for the Logout action. ASP.NET Core supports multiple authentication schemes simultaneously. For our sample, we're supporting both cookies and a scheme called "Auth0" (we could have easily named it something more generic, like "OIDC"). When the user logs out of the application, we want to ensure that awareness of both logins is purged.

There's also a new action called Claims. This action searches through the user identity (which is castable to ClaimsIdentity) for the claim named picture. Once this method finds the picture claim, it puts the value in the ViewData dictionary.

Varying Support for Claims

Not all IDPs are going to give you a claim called picture. Auth0 will give us one if it has been able to figure out the user's picture from the sign-in method (e.g., when users sign in with custom accounts that have email addresses that match registered Gravatars, as in the upcoming example).

Always make sure you get a list of all of the claims guaranteed to be available from your IDP before you write any code that relies on those claims.

Example 10-4 contains the code for the Claims view that iterates through the claims collection and renders the claim type and value in a table, as well as displaying the user's picture.

Example 10-4. Claims.cshtml

```
<div class="row">
    <div class="col-md-12">

        <h3>Current User Claims</h3>

        <br/>
        <img src="@ViewData["picture"]" height="64" width="64"/><br/>

        <table class="table">
            <thead>
                <tr>
                    <th>Claim</th><th>Value</th>
                </tr>
            </thead>
            <tbody>
                @foreach (var claim in User.Claims)
                {
                    <tr>
                        <td>@claim.Type</td>
                        <td>@claim.Value</td>
                    </tr>
                }
            </tbody>
        </table>
    </div>
</div>
```

And finally, Figure 10-2 shows what the */Account/Claims* page looks like when I log in to the application with an account bearing my email address.

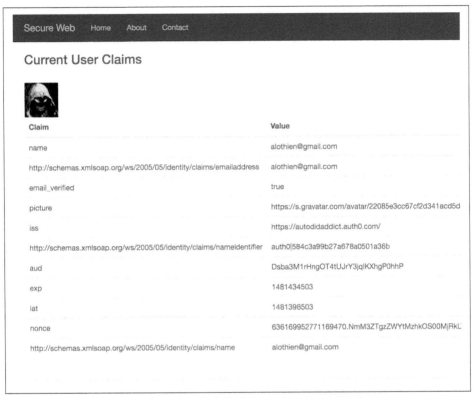

Figure 10-2. Enumerating claims in an OIDC-secured web application

At this point we've gone from the empty scaffolding of an ASP.NET Core web application and connected it to a cloud-friendly third-party identity provider. This relieves our application of the burden of manually managing authentication and allows us to take advantage of bearer tokens and the OIDC standard.

While I normally advocate *avoiding* scaffolding and templates because of their long-storied history of bloat, in this case it wasn't so bad because the template contained stylesheets and layouts we would have had to create anyway.

OIDC Middleware and Cloud Native

I've mentioned a few times how reliance on OS-specific security features will end up causing you a lot of problems in the cloud. There are a number of things that can cause problems when trying to run an application on an elastically scaling platform, and even our shiny new OIDC middleware is subject to some of these issues.

If you're not running this application on Windows, then you might have seen a warning message that looks something like this during startup:

```
warn: Microsoft.Extensions.DependencyInjection.DataProtectionServices[59]
      Neither user profile nor HKLM registry available.
      Using an ephemeral key repository.
       Protected data will be unavailable when application exits.
warn: Microsoft.AspNetCore.DataProtection.Repositories.EphemeralXmlRepository[50]
      Using an in-memory repository.
      Keys will not be persisted to storage.
```

The core of this problem is the use of encryption keys and data protection. In the traditional world of big, bloated Windows servers for .NET applications, we could rely on things like the OS for managing encryption keys.

Imagine that instead of running 1 instance of this application on your laptop, you're running 20 instances of it in the cloud. Unauthenticated users hit instance 1 with no code or token. They get redirected to the IDP, and when they come back to the application they hit instance 2. If information used in the OIDC flow is encrypted by instance 1 and cannot be decrypted by instance 2, you're going to have some catastrophic application failures at runtime.

The solution is to treat the storage and retrieval of security keys as a backing service. There are a number of third-party products, like Vault, that specialize in this functionality, or you can use a distributed cache like Redis and store short-lived keys there.

You've already seen how to use the Steeltoe libraries for application configuration and service discovery when working with the Netflix OSS stack. You can also use a NuGet module from Steeltoe called `Steeltoe.Security.DataProtection.Redis`. This module is designed specifically to move the storage used by the data protection APIs off of the local disk (which is not cloud native) and into an external Redis distributed cache.

Using this library, we can configure external data protection in our `Startup` class's `ConfigureServices` method as follows:

```
services.AddMvc();

services.AddRedisConnectionMultiplexer(Configuration);
services.AddDataProtection()
        .PersistKeysToRedis()
        .SetApplicationName("myapp-redis-keystore");

services.AddDistributedRedisCache(Configuration);

services.AddSession();
```

And then we just call `app.UseSession()` in our `Configure` method to finish setting up external session state.

To see this in action without the rest of the security integration in this chapter, check out the sample in the Steeltoe GitHub repository (*http://bit.ly/2fcdKsD*).

Securing ASP.NET Core Microservices

Securing a microservice with no UI (usually called "headless") automatically rules out any authentication flow that requires direct interaction with a user or a browser capable of facilitating a redirection flow.

In this section, we'll talk about the options available for securing microservices and we'll illustrate one of these options by building a secured service with bearer tokens.

Securing a Service with the Full OIDC Security Flow

One commonly used option for securing a service that supports an OIDC-secured website is to simply implement one of the OIDC authentication flows designed specifically for services.

In this flow, illustrated in Figure 10-3, the user goes through the authentication flow we've already discussed, using browser redirects and interaction with the website and IDP. Once the website establishes a validated claims identity, it will then request an *access token* from the IDP by presenting the identity token as well as information about the desired resource.

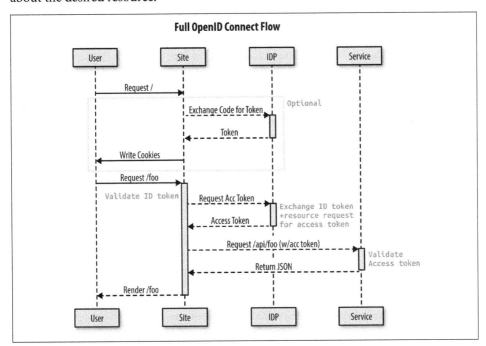

Figure 10-3. OpenID Connect flow securing site and backing service

Essentially, the site will be asking the IDP, "Can user X access resource Y? If so, give me a token asserting this." The token we get back can be validated by a service. If the access token presented by the site doesn't grant the user the permission to do what is desired with the resource in question, the service will reject the HTTP call with a 401 Unauthorized or a 403 Forbidden.

If you don't need every single service call to come embedded with the concept of an interactive user as well as whether or not that person has read or write access to the resource, then this authorization flow may be more than you need. A major disadvantage.

The first is that every single access token requires validation. Some of this can be done simply by opening up the token, but in many scenarios the access token is sent directly to the IDP for verification. This makes the IDP an even more integral part of every transaction flowing through your system, which also makes it qualify as a risk and central point of failure.

It's up to you whether you adopt this strategy, but if you just need to know if the consuming application (be it a service or GUI) is permitted to make calls against the backing service API, then there is a much simpler approach that I'll cover next.

Securing a Service with Client Credentials

The client credentials pattern is one of the simplest ways to secure a service. First, you communicate with the service only via SSL, and second, the code consuming the service is responsible for transmitting credentials. These credentials are usually just called a username and password, or, more appropriate for scenarios that don't involve human interaction, a client key and a client secret. Any time you're looking at a public API hosted in the cloud that requires you to supply a client key and secret, you're looking at an implementation of the client credentials pattern.

It is also fairly common to see the client key and secret transmitted in the form of custom HTTP headers that begin with the X- prefix; e.g., X-MyApp-ClientSecret and X-MyApp-ClientKey.

The code to implement this kind of security is actually pretty simple, so we'll skip the sample here. There are, however, a number of downsides to this solution that stem from its simplicity.

For example, what do you do if a particular client starts abusing the system? Can you disable its access? What if a set of clients appear to be attempting a denial of service attack? Can you block all of them? Perhaps the scariest scenario is this: what happens if a client secret and key are compromised and the consumer gains access to confidential information *without* triggering any behavioral alerts that might get them banned?

What we need is something that combines the simplicity of portable credentials that do not require communication with a third party for validation with some of the

more practical security features of OpenID Connect, like validation of issuers, validation of audience (target), expiring tokens, and more.

Securing a Service with Bearer Tokens

Through our exploration of OpenID Connect, we've already seen that the ability to
transmit portable, independently verifiable tokens is the key technology underpin-
ning all of its authentication flows.

Bearer tokens, specifically those adhering to the JSON Web Token specification, can
also be used independently of OIDC to secure services without involving any browser
redirects or the implicit assumption of human consumers.

The OIDC middleware we used earlier in the chapter builds on top of JWT middleware that we get from the `Microsoft.AspNetCore.Authentication.JwtBearer`
NuGet package.

To use this middleware to secure our service, we can first create an empty service
using any of the previous examples in this book as reference material or scaffolding.
Next, we add a reference to the JWT bearer authentication NuGet package.

In our service's `Startup` class, in the `Configure` method we can enable and configure
JWT bearer authentication, as shown in Example 10-5.

Example 10-5. Startup.cs

```
app.UseJwtBearerAuthentication(new JwtBearerOptions
{
    AutomaticAuthenticate = true,
    AutomaticChallenge = true,
    TokenValidationParameters = new TokenValidationParameters
    {
        ValidateIssuerSigningKey = true,
        IssuerSigningKey = signingKey,
        ValidateIssuer = false,
        ValidIssuer = "https://fake.issuer.com",

        ValidateAudience = false,
        ValidAudience = "https://sampleservice.example.com",

        ValidateLifetime = true,
    }
});
```

We can control all of the different types of things we validate when receiving bearer
tokens, including the issuer's signing key, the issuer, the audience, and the token lifetime. Validation of things like token lifetime usually also requires us to set up options

like allowing some range to accommodate clock skew between token issuer and the secured service.

In the preceding code, we've got validation turned off for issuer and audience, but these are both fairly simple string comparison checks. When we validate these, the issuer and the audience must match *exactly* the issuer and audience contained in the token.

Let's say our service is a stock management service running in support of a store called *alienshoesfrommars.com*. We might see an issuer value of `https://idp.alienshoesfrommars.com` and the audience would be the service itself, `https://stockservice.fulfillment.alienshoesfrommars.com`. While convention dictates that the issuer and audience are both URLs, they do not need to be live websites that respond to requests in order to validate the token.

You may have noticed that we *are* validating the issuer signing key. This is basically the only way that we can ensure that a bearer token was issued by a known and trusted issuer. To create a signing key that we want to match the one that was used to sign the token, we take a secret key (some string) and create a `SymmetricSecurityKey` from it, as shown here:

```
string SecretKey = "seriouslyneverleavethissittinginyourcode";
SymmetricSecurityKey signingKey =
  new SymmetricSecurityKey(
    Encoding.ASCII.GetBytes(SecretKey));
```

As the string indicates, you should *never store the secret key directly in your code*. This should come from an environment variable or some other external product like Vault or a distributed cache like Redis. An attacker who is able to obtain this secret key will be able to fabricate bearer tokens at will and have unfettered access to your no-longer-secure microservices.

Security and Key Rotation

If the keys used to sign your bearer tokens change every couple of minutes or every hour, then even if someone were to be able to capture this key and fabricate tokens, they would only be able to do so for a short period of time.

Both off-the-shelf and custom-built products usually contain some strategy for keeping a shallow key history around so that validators can check bearer tokens against the current key as well as the previous key, or a consumer retry is built into the client code that fetches a new key upon getting a 401 or 403 from a service.

An intruder gaining access to your system may be inevitable, but using techniques like key rotation, short token expiration periods, and minimal allowances for clock

---

skew can mitigate the risk or eliminate the damage someone can do with captured keys.

That's pretty much all we need to start securing our services with bearer tokens. All we need to do is drop the [Authorize] attribute on controller methods that need this, and the JWT validation middleware will be invoked for those methods. Undecorated methods will allow unauthenticated access by default (though you can change this behavior as well).

To consume our secured service, we can create a simple console application that creates a JwtSecurityToken instance from an array of Claim objects, then sends those as an Authorization header bearer token:

```
var claims = new[]
{
    new Claim(JwtRegisteredClaimNames.Sub, "AppUser_Bob"),
    new Claim(JwtRegisteredClaimNames.Jti,
        Guid.NewGuid().ToString()),
    new Claim(JwtRegisteredClaimNames.Iat,
        ToUnixEpochDate(DateTime.Now).ToString(),
        ClaimValueTypes.Integer64),
};

var jwt = new JwtSecurityToken(
    issuer: "issuer",
    audience: "audience",
    claims: claims,
    notBefore: DateTime.UtcNow,
    expires: DateTime.UtcNow.Add(TimeSpan.FromMinutes(20)),
    signingCredentials: creds);

var encodedJwt = new JwtSecurityTokenHandler().WriteToken(jwt);

httpClient.DefaultRequestHeaders.Authorization =
        new AuthenticationHeaderValue("Bearer", encodedJwt);

var result = httpClient.GetAsync("http://localhost:5000/api/secured").Result;
Console.WriteLine(result.StatusCode);
Console.WriteLine(result.Content.ToString());
```

Here's a secured controller method in our service that enumerates the claims sent by the client. Note that this code would never even be executed if the bearer token hadn't already been validated according to our middleware configuration:

```
[Authorize]
[HttpGet]
public string Get()
{
    foreach (var claim in HttpContext.User.Claims) {
        Console.WriteLine($"{claim.Type}:{claim.Value}");
    }
    return "This is from the super secret area";
}
```

Since the JWT validation middleware has already been written for us, there's very little work for us to do in order to support bearer token security for our services. If we want to have more control over which clients can call which controller methods, we can take advantage of the concept of a *policy*. Policies are just custom bits of code that are executed as predicates while determining authorization.

For example, we could define a policy called CheeseburgerPolicy and create a secured controller method that not only requires a valid bearer token, but it also requires that said token meets the criteria defined by the policy:

```
[Authorize( Policy = "CheeseburgerPolicy")]
[HttpGet("policy")]
public string GetWithPolicy()
{
 return "This is from the super secret area w/policy enforcement.";
}
```

Configuring this policy is done easily in the ConfigureServices method. In the following sample, we create CheeseburgerPolicy as a policy that requires a specific claim (icanhazcheeseburger) and value (true):

```
public void ConfigureServices(IServiceCollection services)
{
    services.AddMvc();
    services.AddOptions();

    services.AddAuthorization( options => {
      options.AddPolicy("CheeseburgerPolicy",
          policy =>
             policy.RequireClaim("icanhazcheeseburger", "true"));
    });
}
```

Now if we modify our console application to add a new claim of this type with a value of true, we will be able to invoke regular secured controller methods as well as controller methods secured with the CheeseburgerPolicy.

The policy can require specific claims, usernames, assertions, or roles. You can also define your own requirement that implements IAuthorizationRequirement so that you can add your own validation logic while not polluting your individual controllers.

Summary

Security isn't an afterthought. It's also something that cannot be condensed into a single chapter with complete coverage. This chapter provided you with some basic guidance around securing web applications with OIDC and how to secure microservices with JWT bearer token technology.

In both cases the middleware is already written for us, so all we had to do was figure out how to configure and invoke the appropriate code and understand how the various security technologies work. If you have more than a passing interest in identity and secure communications in the cloud, I strongly suggest that you check out some books and online references on the subject.

CHAPTER 11

Building Real-Time Apps and Services

Throughout the book we have been looking at various ways microservices accept input and produce output. We've seen the traditional RESTful services and we've seen services that consume and produce messages in queues.

Users of modern web and mobile applications often demand more than the eventual consistency we discussed in Chapter 6 (ES/CQRS). They want to know about things that are important to them, and they want to know about them immediately.

This brings us to the topic of this chapter: *real-time services*. This chapter will discuss what the phrase "real-time" means and the types of applications most consumers consider to be within that category. Then we'll look at websockets and how traditional websocket programming models fall short in the cloud, and build a sample real-time application that demonstrates the power of adding real-time messaging to an event-sourced system.

Real-Time Applications Defined

Before we can define a real-time application we need to define real-time. Just like the term *microservices*, *real-time* is overloaded, overused, and usually has at least two different meanings for every person in the room discussing it.

Definithing.com defines it as:

> A term used to describe computer systems that update information at the same rate as they receive data.

Other definitions of real-time suggest that something is real-time if it can process input and produce output within a few milliseconds. To me this seems like a fairly arbitrary value. Some systems with ultra-low latency requirements might consider real-time to be a processing time of a few hundred *microseconds*, not milliseconds.

The event processor we created in Chapter 6 is more than capable of processing input (member location events), detecting proximity, and emitting proximity detected events within a few milliseconds. By either of the definitions we've covered so far, our location event processor can be considered a real-time system.

I think a slightly broader definition of real-time might be to say that events occur with little to no delay between receipt and processing. The definition of "little" here has to be one that is agreed upon by the development team based on the system requirements and application domain and can't be some arbitrary value of some randomly chosen unit of measure.

One source says that examples of real-time applications might be a missile guidance system or an airline booking application. I can completely understand the real-time nature of a missile guidance system—an embedded processor performing millions of calculations per second based on input from dozens or hundreds of sensors in order to control the flight of a projectile and report feedback to the ground. Other real-time applications that fall into a similar category might be autonomous cars, hobby and commercial drone autopilot software, and pattern recognition software applied to live video feeds.

But what about an airline booking system? I think this is a step too far. Most of us have experienced the eventual consistency (or *rarely consistent*) nature of these systems. You can book a ticket, and your mobile device might take 24 hours to receive your boarding pass. You may get notifications of a flight delay or gate change an hour after that information might have been relevant to you. There are exceptions of course, but for a large number of cases, these are *batch mode* systems and *time-polling* systems that rarely exhibit the traits of a real-time application.

This brings up another anti-pattern of real-time systems. Here are some characteristics of applications that disqualify them from the real-time category:

- Your application collects input and waits before producing output.
- Your application only produces output on timed intervals or upon external stimuli that occur on any kind of schedule or are random in nature.

A really common trait or characteristic of real-time systems is that interested parties are notified of events concerning them via *push notification*, rather than the interested party performing a poll or timed query to check for updates. We're going to be talking about push notifications of various kinds throughout the rest of the chapter.

Websockets in the Cloud

We've already covered one form of messaging extensively throughout this book—the use of message queues via a messaging server like RabbitMQ. When developers think about *real-time* applications, one thing that often comes to mind is the use of websockets to *push* data and notifications to a live (real-time) web-based UI.

Just a few years ago, using a website that would update and react to you dynamically would have seemed remarkable and been labeled as "the future." Nowadays we take this kind of thing for granted.

When we go to a website that sells products, we take it as given that we should be able to have a live chat with support people. It's no big surprise when Facebook pops up notifications letting us know that someone's commented on our post or we see the site change and react dynamically when someone retweets one of our tweets.

While not all of this functionality is supported explicitly through websockets, most of it was a few years ago and much of it is still supported through either websockets or something designed to appear like a websocket to developers.

The WebSocket Protocol

The WebSocket protocol showed up around 2008 and defines the means by which a persistent, bidirectional socket connection can be made between a browser and a server. This allows data to be sent to a server from a web application running in the browser, and it allows a server to send data down without requiring the application to "poll" (periodically check for updates, usually on a sliding/exponential fall-off scale).

At a low level, the browser requests a connection *upgrade* of the server. Once the handshake finishes, the browser and server switch to a separate, *binary* TCP connection for bidirectional communication.

From the specification (*https://tools.ietf.org/html/rfc6455*), and the corresponding Wikipedia page (*https://en.wikipedia.org/wiki/WebSocket*), an HTTP request asking for a connection upgrade looks something like this:

```
GET /chat HTTP/1.1
Host: server.example.com
Upgrade: websocket
Connection: Upgrade
Sec-WebSocket-Key: x3JJHMbDL1EzLkh9GBhXDw==
Sec-WebSocket-Protocol: chat, superchat
Sec-WebSocket-Version: 13
Origin: http://example.com
```

The websockets are then used to do everything from pushing pop-up notifications on social media websites to updating live, streaming dashboards and monitoring consoles and even playing interactive multiplayer games with little more than HTML and clever use of graphics and CSS.

Deployment Models

What does any of this have to do with the cloud? In a traditional deployment model, you spin up a server (physical or virtual), you install your hosting product (an IIS web server or some J2EE container like WebSphere, for example) and then you deploy your application. If your application is scalable and works on a farm, you then repeat this process over again for each server in your farm or cluster.

When a user connects to a page on your site that opens a websocket connection, that connection stays open with whatever server was chosen to handle the initial request. Until the user hits refresh or clicks another link, that websocket should work just fine, though there are other issues that might come up with proxies and firewalls.

Let's say now that all of your servers are running on EC2 instances in AWS. When a cloud-based infrastructure is hosting your virtual machines, they are subject to relocation, destruction, and reconstruction at any moment. This is a *good thing*, and designed to allow your application to scale virtually without limit. Unfortunately, this means that these "live" websocket connections can be broken or become stale and unresponsive without notice.

Furthermore, the use of always-up TCP connections to individual servers can impact your own application's ability to scale. Depending on the volume of requests and data your application code is servicing, also managing these connections and the data exchange for them can become a troublesome burden.

The solution here is usually to externalize the use of websockets—to offload the management of websocket connections and data transfer to something that exists (and scales) outside your application code. Another solution that helps with scaling is avoiding websockets entirely and using HTTP-based messaging systems.

In short, rather than your application managing websockets on its own, you should let the experts manage websockets and use a cloud messaging provider. It's worth remembering that you're building an application for your business; you're not (usually) planning on specializing in the art of websocket management.

Whether you host your own cloud messaging server within your infrastructure or your use a separate messaging provider hosted elsewhere in the cloud is up to you and will depend on your requirements and business domain.

Using a Cloud Messaging Provider

We know that we want our application to have real-time capabilities. We want our microservices to be able to push data down to clients, knowing that those clients will not have a live TCP connection to the microservice. We also want applications to be able to use the same or a similar message pipeline to send messages into our back-end.

In order for our microservices to remain cloud native and retain the ability to scale and move around freely in the cloud, we need to pick a messaging provider to manage some of our real-time capabilities out of process.

The list of companies that provide messaging services is enormous and growing every day. The following are just a few of the many companies that offer cloud messaging either as a standalone product or as part of a larger suite of services:

- **Apigee** (API gateway and real-time messaging)
- **PubNub** (real-time messaging and presence)
- **Pusher** (real-time messaging and presence)
- **Kaazing** (real-time messaging)
- **Mashery** (API gateway and real-time messaging)
- **Google** (Google Cloud Messaging)
- **ASP.NET SignalR** (real-time messaging hosted in Azure)
- **Amazon** (Simple Notification Service)

The criteria you use to select your messaging provider will be based entirely on your needs, the type of application you're building, budget, expected volume, whether you're incorporating mobile devices or IoT components, and so on.

Regardless of which mechanism you choose, you should invest a little time in insulating your code from the exact provider so that you can change this without having too much of a far-reaching impact. An anti-corruption layer (ACL) would be a pretty good recommendation here to insulate your app from implementation models from specific providers bleeding into your codebase.

In this chapter, we're going to use *PubNub*. I chose it somewhat arbitrarily, but also because of the simple SDK, excellent documentation, ready availability of public samples, and the fact that we can use it for demonstration purposes without having to hand over a credit card number.

Building the Proximity Monitor

In Chapter 6, in the course of our discussion of Event Sourcing and the Command Query Responsibility Segregation pattern, we built an application made up of multiple microservices that detected whenever teammates moved within range of each other.

When this system detects two nearby teammates, it emits a `ProximityDetectedEvent` onto a queue—but that's where we stopped designing and coding. What we want to do now is build a monitor that updates *in real time* whenever the backend system detects one of these proximity events.

For the purposes of our example, we'll be keeping the UI to something simple, but it shouldn't take much imagination to envision some of the potential real-time user interfaces that might be possible here. We could create a maps integration where the current positions of all of the team members are plotted, and we might bounce or animate team members' avatars when the system has detected that they are within range of each other. These team members might also receive notifications on their mobile devices at the same time.

Creating a Proximity Monitor Service

Our proximity monitor sample will have a couple of different components. The first thing that we want to do is consume the `ProximityDetectedEvent` that comes off of the queue from the services written in Chapter 6.

Once we do that, we want to grab the raw information on this event and make calls to the team service (written earlier in the book as well) to grab user-friendly information like team and member names. Finally, once we've obtained this augmented data, we want to send a new message out on our real-time messaging system (in our case, this will be PubNub).

The code for the entire proximity monitor is available on GitHub (*http://bit.ly/ 2vbe6Di*).

In another implementation of a pattern used a few times in this book, we're going to create a broad-scoped *processor* class. This class will have a bunch of other subordinate utilities injected into it. The single main "processing" function of this class should read almost like documentation of the high-level logic flow gleaned from our requirements.

Example 11-1 shows the code for our `ProximityDetectedEventProcessor`, the high-level coordinator behind the proximity monitor.

Example 11-1. ProximityDetectedEventProcessor.cs

```
using System;
using Microsoft.Extensions.Logging;
using Microsoft.Extensions.Options;
using StatlerWaldorfCorp.ProximityMonitor.Queues;
using StatlerWaldorfCorp.ProximityMonitor.Realtime;
using StatlerWaldorfCorp.ProximityMonitor.TeamService;

namespace StatlerWaldorfCorp.ProximityMonitor.Events
{
public class ProximityDetectedEventProcessor : IEventProcessor
{
    private ILogger logger;
    private IRealtimePublisher publisher;
    private IEventSubscriber subscriber;

    private PubnubOptions pubnubOptions;
```

```
public ProximityDetectedEventProcessor(
    ILogger<ProximityDetectedEventProcessor> logger,
    IRealtimePublisher publisher,
    IEventSubscriber subscriber,
    ITeamServiceClient teamClient,
    IOptions<PubnubOptions> pubnubOptions)
{
    this.logger = logger;
    this.pubnubOptions = pubnubOptions.Value;
    this.publisher = publisher;
    this.subscriber = subscriber;

    logger.LogInformation("Created Proximity Event Processor.");

    subscriber.ProximityDetectedEventReceived += (pde) => {
      Team t = teamClient.GetTeam(pde.TeamID);
      Member sourceMember =
          teamClient.GetMember(pde.TeamID, pde.SourceMemberID);
      Member targetMember =
          teamClient.GetMember(pde.TeamID, pde.TargetMemberID);

      ProximityDetectedRealtimeEvent outEvent =
      new ProximityDetectedRealtimeEvent
      {
          TargetMemberID = pde.TargetMemberID,
          SourceMemberID = pde.SourceMemberID,
          DetectionTime = pde.DetectionTime,
          SourceMemberLocation = pde.SourceMemberLocation,
          TargetMemberLocation = pde.TargetMemberLocation,
          MemberDistance = pde.MemberDistance,
          TeamID = pde.TeamID,
          TeamName = t.Name,
          SourceMemberName =
            $"{sourceMember.FirstName} {sourceMember.LastName}",
          TargetMemberName =
            $"{targetMember.FirstName} {targetMember.LastName}"
        };
      publisher.Publish(
        this.pubnubOptions.ProximityEventChannel,
        outEvent.toJson());
    };
}

public void Start()
{
    subscriber.Subscribe();
}

public void Stop()
{
    subscriber.Unsubscribe();
```

```
        }
    }
}
```

The first thing to notice in this code listing is the long list of dependencies that we'll be injecting into the constructor from the DI service provider:

- Logger
- Real-time event publisher
- Event subscriber (queue-based)
- Team service client
- PubNub options

The logger is self-explanatory. The real-time event publisher, a class that conforms to the `IRealtimePublisher` interface, allows us to publish a string message on a given channel (also specified by a string). We will be publishing events of type `Proxim ityDetectedRealtimeEvent` on this channel, serializing the data into JSON.

The event subscriber listens to our queue (RabbitMQ), awaiting messages of type `ProximityDetectedEvent`. When we start and stop our event processor, we subscribe and unsubscribe the event subscriber accordingly.

The team service client is used to query the team service for team and member details. We use the team and member service details to populate the member properties (first and last name) and the team name property on the real-time event.

Finally, the PubNub options class holds information like the name of the channel on which the message will be published. While our underlying implementation is PubNub, the vast majority of cloud messaging providers have some concept of a channel for message publishing, so we should be relatively safe swapping PubNub out for a different provider if we choose.

Creating a real-time publisher class

A good refactor for the future might be to create another small class that is responsible for creating a new instance of a `ProximityDetectedRealtimeEvent` class from every `ProximityDetectedEvent` received. This is not just an anti-corruption function, but also augmentation that grabs the team member's name and other user-friendly information. From a functional purist's perspective, this code doesn't really belong in the high-level processor, but rather should be delegated to a supporting tool that's been tested in isolation.

Moving on from the high-level processor, let's take a look at the implementation of our `IRealtimePublisher` interface in Example 11-2, one that uses the PubNub API.

Example 11-2. PubnubRealtimePublisher.cs

```csharp
using Microsoft.Extensions.Logging;
using PubnubApi;

namespace StatlerWaldorfCorp.ProximityMonitor.Realtime
{
public class PubnubRealtimePublisher : IRealtimePublisher
{
    private ILogger logger;

    private Pubnub pubnubClient;

    public PubnubRealtimePublisher(
        ILogger<PubnubRealtimePublisher> logger,
        Pubnub pubnubClient)
    {
        logger.LogInformation(
          "Realtime Publisher (Pubnub) Created.");
        this.logger = logger;
        this.pubnubClient = pubnubClient;
    }

    public void Validate()
    {
        pubnubClient.Time()
          .Async(new PNTimeResultExt(
          (result, status) => {
            if (status.Error) {
              logger.LogError(
               $"Unable to connect to Pubnub {status.ErrorData.Information}");
               throw status.ErrorData.Throwable;
              } else {
              logger.LogInformation("Pubnub connection established.");
              }
          }
        ));
    }

    public void Publish(string channelName, string message)
    {
      pubnubClient.Publish()
        .Channel(channelName)
        .Message(message)
        .Async(new PNPublishResultExt(
          (result, status) => {
             if (status.Error) {
                logger.LogError(
            $"Failed to publish on channel {channelName}:
              {status.ErrorData.Information}");
              } else {
                logger.LogInformation(
```

```
        $"Published message on channel {channelName}, {status.AffectedChannels.Count}
          affected channels, code: {status.StatusCode}");
            }
        }
    ));
    }
 }
}
```

The code here is pretty straightforward. It is just a simple wrapper around the Pub-
Nub SDK (*https://www.pubnub.com/docs/dot-net/pubnub-c-sharp-sdk-v4*). The
instance of the Pubnub class from the SDK is configured through some extensions I
wrote that register a factory with ASP.NET Core.

Injecting the real-time classes

You can see how the Pubnub client and other classes are enabled through DI in
the Startup class in Example 11-3.

Example 11-3. Startup.cs

```
using Microsoft.AspNetCore.Builder;
using Microsoft.AspNetCore.Hosting;
using Microsoft.Extensions.Configuration;
using Microsoft.Extensions.DependencyInjection;
using Microsoft.Extensions.Logging;
using StatlerWaldorfCorp.ProximityMonitor.Queues;
using StatlerWaldorfCorp.ProximityMonitor.Realtime;
using RabbitMQ.Client.Events;
using StatlerWaldorfCorp.ProximityMonitor.Events;
using Microsoft.Extensions.Options;
using RabbitMQ.Client;
using StatlerWaldorfCorp.ProximityMonitor.TeamService;

namespace StatlerWaldorfCorp.ProximityMonitor
{
    public class Startup
    {
        public Startup(IHostingEnvironment env,
          ILoggerFactory loggerFactory)
        {
            loggerFactory.AddConsole();
            loggerFactory.AddDebug();

            var builder = new ConfigurationBuilder()
                .SetBasePath(env.ContentRootPath)
                .AddJsonFile("appsettings.json",
                optional: false, reloadOnChange: false)
                .AddEnvironmentVariables();
```

```
    Configuration = builder.Build();
}


public IConfigurationRoot Configuration { get; }


public void ConfigureServices(
  IServiceCollection services)
{
    services.AddMvc();
    services.AddOptions();

    services.Configure<QueueOptions>(
      Configuration.GetSection("QueueOptions"));
    services.Configure<PubnubOptions>(
      Configuration.GetSection("PubnubOptions"));
    services.Configure<TeamServiceOptions>(
      Configuration.GetSection("teamservice"));
    services.Configure<AMQPOptions>(
      Configuration.GetSection("amqp"));

    services.AddTransient(typeof(IConnectionFactory),
      typeof(AMQPConnectionFactory));
    services.AddTransient(typeof(EventingBasicConsumer),
      typeof(RabbitMQEventingConsumer));
    services.AddSingleton(typeof(IEventSubscriber),
      typeof(RabbitMQEventSubscriber));
    services.AddSingleton(typeof(IEventProcessor),
      typeof(ProximityDetectedEventProcessor));
    services.AddTransient(typeof(ITeamServiceClient),
      typeof(HttpTeamServiceClient));

    services.AddRealtimeService();
    services.AddSingleton(typeof(IRealtimePublisher),
      typeof(PubnubRealtimePublisher));
}

public void Configure(IApplicationBuilder app,
        IHostingEnvironment env,
        ILoggerFactory loggerFactory,
        IEventProcessor eventProcessor,
        IOptions<PubnubOptions> pubnubOptions,
        IRealtimePublisher realtimePublisher)
{
    realtimePublisher.Validate();
    realtimePublisher.Publish(
      pubnubOptions.Value.StartupChannel,
        "{'hello': 'world'}");

    eventProcessor.Start();
```

```
        app.UseMvc();
    }
  }
}
```

The `AddRealtimeService` method is a static extension method that I created to simplify the injection of the implementation of an `IRealtimePublisher` by the service
provider.

So far in the book we've been using only the simplest and most basic features of
ASP.NET Core's dependency injection. What we're trying to do now is make sure that
we can create a class (like the `PubnubRealtimePublisher`) that can have a ready-made
instance of the PubNub API injected into it.

To do this cleanly and still allow all of our configuration to be injected, including the
secret API keys, we need to register a *factory*. The factory is going to be a class that
dispenses configured instances of the Pubnub class from the PubNub SDK.

Example 11-4 shows the relatively simple factory class.

Example 11-4. PubnubFactory.cs

```
using Microsoft.Extensions.Options;
using PubnubApi;
using Microsoft.Extensions.Logging;

namespace StatlerWaldorfCorp.ProximityMonitor.Realtime
{
public class PubnubFactory
{
    private PNConfiguration pnConfiguration;

    private ILogger logger;

    public PubnubFactory(IOptions<PubnubOptions> pubnubOptions,
        ILogger<PubnubFactory> logger)
    {
        this.logger = logger;

        pnConfiguration = new PNConfiguration();
        pnConfiguration.PublishKey =
            pubnubOptions.Value.PublishKey;
        pnConfiguration.SubscribeKey =
            pubnubOptions.Value.SubscribeKey;
        pnConfiguration.Secure = false;
    }

    public Pubnub CreateInstance()
    {
        return new Pubnub(pnConfiguration);
```

```
            }
    }
}
```

Given PubNub options (we have these in our *appsettings.json* file, which can be overridden via environment variables), this class creates a new instance of the Pubnub class. The real trick, and the code that will likely come in handy in your development projects, is the static extension method to plug this factory into the DI mechanism, shown in Example 11-5.

Example 11-5. RealtimeServiceCollectionExtensions.cs

```
using System;
using Microsoft.Extensions.DependencyInjection;
using PubnubApi;

namespace StatlerWaldorfCorp.ProximityMonitor.Realtime
{
public static class RealtimeServiceCollectionExtensions
{
    public static IServiceCollection AddRealtimeService(
        this IServiceCollection services)
    {
        services.AddTransient<PubnubFactory>();

        return AddInternal(services,
          p => p.GetRequiredService<PubnubFactory>(),
          ServiceLifetime.Singleton);
    }

    private static IServiceCollection AddInternal(
        this IServiceCollection collection,
        Func<IServiceProvider, PubnubFactory> factoryProvider,
        ServiceLifetime lifetime)
    {
        Func<IServiceProvider, object> factoryFunc = provider =>
        {
            var factory = factoryProvider(provider);
            return factory.CreateInstance();
        };

        var descriptor = new ServiceDescriptor(
            typeof(Pubnub),
            factoryFunc, lifetime);
        collection.Add(descriptor);
        return collection;
    }
}
}
```

A good rule of thumb when trying to work within the constraints of a DI system is to ask yourself what your class needs to work. If it needs a thing that you cannot yet inject, create something (a wrapper, perhaps) that allows it to be injectable, and then reevaluate. This process usually results in several small wrapper classes but a pretty clean and easy-to-follow injection path.

The key bit of work in the preceding code was creating a lambda function that accepts an `IServiceProvider` as input and returns an object as output. This is the *factory function* that we pass into the *service descriptor* when we register the factory.

Hereafter, any time any object requires an instance of a `Pubnub` object, it will be dispensed through the factory we registered in the line:

```
var descriptor = new ServiceDescriptor(
        typeof(Pubnub),
        factoryFunc, lifetime);
```

This descriptor indicates that a request for `Pubnub` will be satisfied by invoking the factory function in the variable `factoryFunc`, with the given object lifetime.

Putting it all together

To see this in action and make sure everything is working, we can fake the output of the services from Chapter 6 by manually dropping a `ProximityDetectedEvent` JSON string into the `proximitydetected` queue, as shown in the following screenshot from the RabbitMQ console (Figure 11-1).

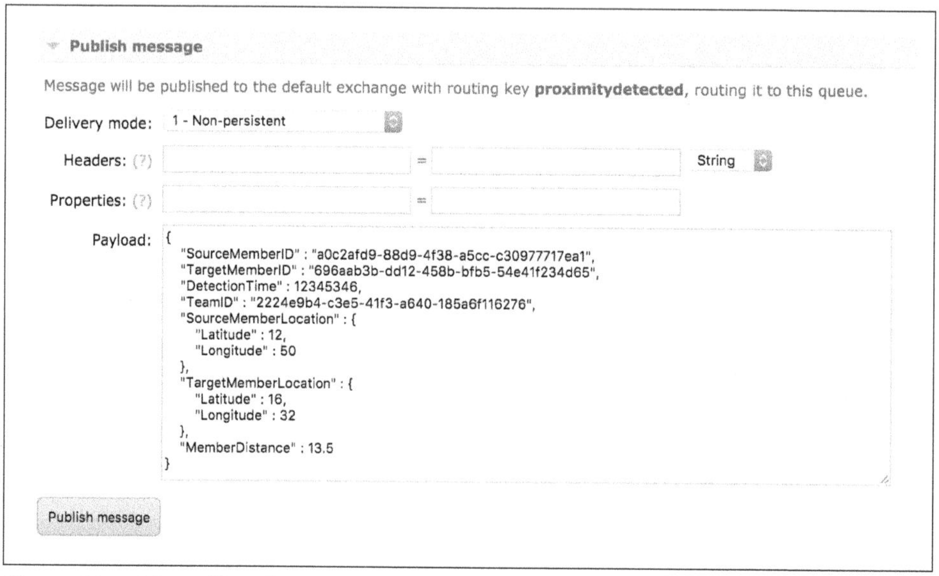

Figure 11-1. Manually submitting a proximity detected event

If our proximity monitor service is running and subscribed to the queue when this happens, and our team service is running and has all the appropriate data in it (there are some sample shell scripts in the GitHub repository that show you how to seed the team service with test data), then the proximity monitor will pick up the event, augment it, and then dispatch a real-time event through PubNub.

Using the PubNub debug console, we can see the output of this process show up immediately (technically it's *almost* immediate) after processing (Figure 11-2).

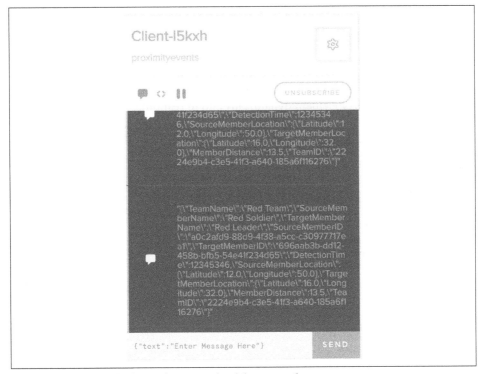

Figure 11-2. PubNub channel view in the debug console

You can copy and modify the script file in the GitHub repository (*http://bit.ly/2vXnRs9*) that populates the team service with sample data as well as a sample JSON file containing a test proximity event so you can run through this yourself without having to start any of the code from Chapter 6.

Creating a Real-Time Proximity Monitor UI

Having a microservice that picks up proximity events, augments them, and then sends them out for dispatch to our real-time messaging system is great, but at this point we haven't done anything meaningful with the real-time message.

As mentioned earlier, we could use this message to move thumbtacks on a map UI, we could dynamically update tables or charts, or we could simply create little toasts or pop-up notifications in a web UI. Depending on our messaging provider, we could also have these messages automatically converted into push notifications and sent directly to team members' mobile devices.

To keep things simple and to hide the fact that I have no artistic skills whatsoever, I'll just use a very simple HTML page that has no graphics and doesn't require a server of any kind.

For a full set of details on how to interact with PubNub messages and channels using JavaScript, please check out their JavaScript SDK documentation (*http://bit.ly/ 2w0Q2nO*).

Example 11-6 is our very simple example that listens for proximity events and adds the information to a div element dynamically and in real time.

Example 11-6. realtimetest.html

```
<html>
<head>
<title>RT page sample</title>
<script src="https://cdn.pubnub.com/sdk/javascript/pubnub.4.4.0.js"></script>
<script>
var pubnub = new PubNub({
    subscribeKey: "yoursubkey",
    publishKey: "yourprivatekey",
    ssl: true
});

pubnub.addListener({
    message: function(m) {
        // handle message
        var channelName = m.channel;
        var channelGroup = m.subscription;
        var pubTT = m.timetoken;
        var msg = JSON.parse(m.message);
        console.log("New Message!!", msg);
        var newDiv = document.createElement('div')
        var newStr = "** (" + msg.TeamName + ") " +
            msg.SourceMemberName + " moved within " +
            msg.MemberDistance + "km of " + msg.TargetMemberName;
        newDiv.innerHTML = newStr
        var oldDiv = document.getElementById('chatLog')
        oldDiv.appendChild(newDiv)
    },
    presence: function(p) {
        // handle presence
    },
    status: function(s) {
```

```
        // handle status
    }
});

console.log("Subscribing..");
pubnub.subscribe({
    channels: ['proximityevents']
});
</script>
</head>
<body>
<h1>Proximity Monitor</h1>
<p>Proximity Events listed below.</p>

<div id="chatLog">
</div>
</body>
</html>
```

Here we have an HTML `div` called `chatLog`. Every time we receive a message from the PubNub channel `proximityevents` we create a new `div` and append it as a child. This new `div` has the name of the team as well as the names of the source and target members, as shown in Figure 11-3.

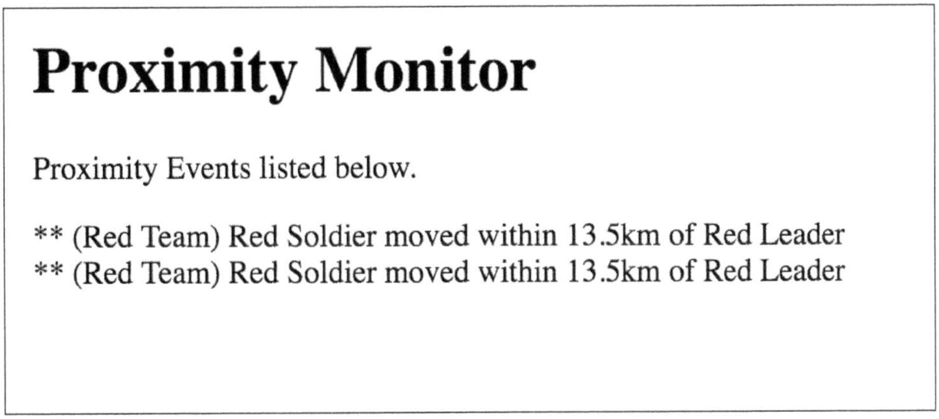

Proximity Monitor

Proximity Events listed below.

** (Red Team) Red Soldier moved within 13.5km of Red Leader
** (Red Team) Red Soldier moved within 13.5km of Red Leader

Figure 11-3. Receiving real-time messages via JavaScript

It's worth pointing out that you don't need to host this file on a server; you can open it in any browser and the JavaScript just runs. When you look at the documentation for PubNub's other SDKs (including mobile), you'll see how easy it is to achieve real-time communication between backend services, end users using web browsers, mobile devices, and other integration points. This ease of use isn't limited to just PubNub, either; most cloud messaging providers (including Amazon, Azure, and Google) have very easy to use SDKs and their documentation is typically rich and full of good examples.

Summary

In this chapter we added some clarity to the definition of *real-time*—what it means and what it doesn't. We also talked about how we've already done some near-real-time programming in this book in Chapter 6, with our use of queues and immediate subscriptions.

This chapter showed you how to build on the knowledge you've accumulated so far to seamlessly integrate third-party cloud messaging providers into your codebase. The use of cloud messaging providers can give you dynamic and real-time-updating UIs for web and desktop as well as enabling fully interactive mobile applications that run on semi-connected devices.

Real-time messaging systems are often the glue that makes the independent components of a highly scalable, distributed, and eventually consistent system work.

There are even messaging providers that have special accommodations for the IoT, so you could use the patterns in this chapter to integrate your army of evil robots (or a smart fridge, whichever you prefer) with your ASP.NET Core backend.

Personally, I would go with the army of robots.

CHAPTER 12

Putting It All Together

I started this book by showing you how to build a console application ("Hello, world!") in Microsoft's new cross-platform development framework, .NET Core. From there, you simply added package references and method calls to gradually progress from a console app to a fully functioning web server capable of hosting RESTful endpoints with the Model–View–Controller pattern fully supported.

While I don't want to belittle the importance of learning syntax and the details of which lines of code to write and when, there is an important lesson to learn here: *code won't solve all your problems.*

Building microservices isn't about learning C#, or Java, or Go—it's about learning how to build applications that thrive in elastically scaling environments, that do not have host affinity, and that can start and stop at a moment's notice. In other words, it's about building *cloud-native* applications.

As we've progressed from chapter to chapter, we've deferred some important discussions in service of explaining the details. Now that we're done with the details, I'd like to use this chapter to revisit some patterns, discuss areas where we may have cut corners, and even present a few philosophical ideas likely to fuel debates that might cause riots within your development team.

Identifying and Fixing Anti-Patterns

Every author has to walk the fine line between providing real-world samples and providing samples that are small and simple enough to digest in the relatively short medium of a single book or chapter.

This is why there are so many "hello world" samples in books: because otherwise you'd have 30 pages of prose and 1,000 pages of code listings. A balance has to be struck, and compromises have to be made in order to focus the reader's attention on solving one problem at a time.

Throughout the book we've made some compromises in order to maintain this balance, but I want to go back now and revisit some ideas and philosophies to help better inform your decision-making process now that you've had a chance to build, run, and tinker with all of the code samples.

Cleaning Up the Team Monitor Sample

You may recall from multiple chapters earlier in the book that we've been building pieces of a large application consisting of multiple microservices.

In this sample, we started with a simple service that managed information about teams and team members. We expanded that concept later to add location tracking with a backing service. Then, in Chapter 6, we built a solution that looks like the diagram in Figure 12-1.

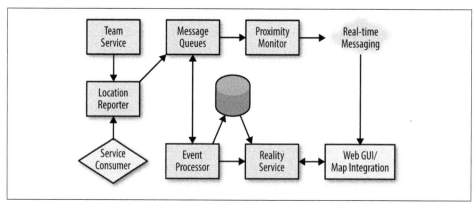

Figure 12-1. Team monitoring solution with anti-patterns

In this more involved scenario, we start with mobile devices submitting the GPS coordinates of team members to the location reporter service. From there, these commands are converted into events with augmented data from the team service. Information then flows through the system, eventually causing notifications of *proximity events* (team members who move within range of each other) to arrive at some consumer-facing interface like a web page or mobile device.

At first glance this looks nice, and it served the purpose of demonstrating the code we wanted to show. But if we look a little bit closer, we'll see that the event processor and the reality service are actually sharing a data store. For our sample, this was a Redis cache.

One of the rules of microservices often quoted during architecture and design meetings is "never use a database as an integration layer." It is an offshoot of the *share nothing* principle. We often talk about this rule but we rarely spend enough time discussing the reasons *why* it's a rule.

One common side effect of using a database as an integration tier is that you end up with two (or more!) services that require a certain data structure or schema to exist in order to function. This means you can no longer change the underlying data store independently, and these services often end up in a lockstep release cadence rather than allowing for independent releases as they should.

While this might not be a problem for Redis, multiple services reading and writing the same data can often cause performance problems due to locking or, worse, can even cause data corruption.

Of course opinions on this vary wildly, so it's entirely up to you to decide whether you think this kind of sharing is viable. For a microservices purist like myself, I would try to avoid any architecture that tightly couples two services to each other, including the sharing of a data store that creates tight coupling to an actual persistence schema.

To correct this problem, we can redesign our architecture as shown in Figure 12-2.

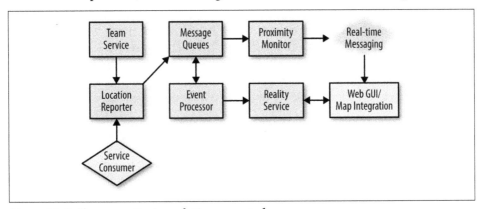

Figure 12-2. Team monitoring solution corrected

In this new design, the event processor and reality service are not using the same data store. In the old design, the event processor wrote the location data directly to the "reality cache" (our Redis server). In the new design, the event processor invokes the reality service, asking it to write the current location.

In this architecture, the reality service is the *sole owner* of the reality cache data. This frees the service up to change its underlying persistence mechanism and schema whenever the team wants, and allows both the reality service and the event processor to remain on independent release cadences so long as they adhere to best practices when it comes to semantic versioning of public APIs.

Another optimization is to allow the reality service to maintain its own private data, but to also maintain an external cache. The external cache would conform to a well-known specification that should be treated like a public API (e.g., breaking changes have downstream consequences). An illustration of this is shown in Figure 12-3.

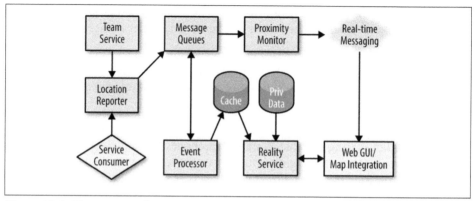

Figure 12-3. Treating a cache as a versioned, public API

We might not need this optimization, but it is just one of many ways around the problem of using a data store as an integration layer between services. There's nothing wrong with using a cache to provide a subset of functionality or as an optimization, so long as the shared cache doesn't become a reason to force different development teams into a lockstep release cadence or create release dependencies.

Continuing the Debate over Composite Microservices

Before we talk about the pros and cons of *composite services*, we should probably define that phrase. A composite service is any service that depends on invoking another service in order to satisfy a request. This is almost always a *synchronous* call, which blocks the original call until one or more nested calls complete.

We've seen this pattern a few times in this book while demonstrating various aspects of ASP.NET Core. First, we saw the pattern when an early version of the team service invoked the location service when a caller asked for details on a specific team member.

Later, we saw this same pattern when discussing service discovery and registration. In Chapter 8, we built a solution that has a data flow like the one illustrated in Figure 12-4.

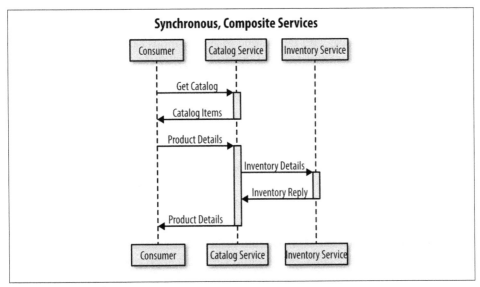

Figure 12-4. Synchronous, composite service usage

In this scenario, a client that requests product details must *wait* while the catalog service makes a synchronous call to the inventory service to fetch the stock status of a particular item.

This is a relatively simple scenario, but let's imagine that this pattern propagates throughout an enterprise. Suppose the inventory service gets modified a few months after release to depend on some new service. That new service then gets split because people think it's "too big." The team that built the original product service might be blissfully unaware that their one seemingly harmless, synchronous call to inventory is now a chain six deep of synchronous calls. Without the product team doing anything, their average response time could have gone from a few hundred milliseconds to longer than a full second.

Worse, in this hypothetical scenario, the failure rate of the product service has skyrocketed. It used to work all the time, and now clients are reporting timeouts and strange server errors. This happens because somewhere in the deeply nested pile of synchronous calls, something fails and that low-level failure creates a cascade that bubbles back up to the client.

There are microservice design purists who firmly believe that a true microservice *should never call another service synchronously*. While I don't think this rule applies to all situations all the time, we should definitely be keenly aware of the risks involved in making synchronous calls out of our services.

Mitigating Risk with Circuit Breakers

One potential way to deal with the nesting of synchronous calls is to come up with a fallback mechanism; a way to deal with failures anywhere in the call chain. The pattern of providing a fallback instead of either crashing or blocking indefinitely in the presence of a failing backing service is usually called implementing a *circuit breaker*.

A full dissertation on circuit breakers and common implementations could potentially take up a book on its own. Microsoft has a decent introductory article (*https:// msdn.microsoft.com/en-us/library/dn589784.aspx*), and you can read more about the original driving philosophy in Martin Fowler's post (*https://martinfowler.com/bliki/ CircuitBreaker.html*). According to Fowler, the circuit breaker pattern was originally popularized in Michael Nygard's book *Release It!* (Pragmatic Press).

When we make calls to other services, those calls can fail. The reasons for these failures are nearly infinite. The service could return unexpected data, causing our process to crash. The service could not respond within an appropriate time, blocking our callers. The network could do all kinds of terrible things to our request, preventing it from being handled.

Rather than letting these failures happen over and over and cause untold destruction, after some threshold is crossed, the circuit breaker is *tripped*. Once it's tripped, we no longer attempt to communicate with the broken service, and we instead return some appropriate fallback value.

Just like in our houses, if a circuit fails for whatever reason (a short, too much current draw, etc.), the circuit breaker trips and power is no longer supplied to the failing circuit for fear of the potential damage that could be caused.

The sequence diagram in Figure 12-5 shows the synchronous flow when the circuit is tripped between the catalog and inventory services.

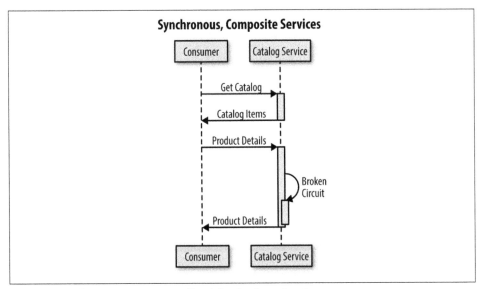

Figure 12-5. Composite service calls with a broken circuit

In this scenario, we never attempt to call the inventory service. Rather than returning live inventory data in the product details, we could simply return "N/A" for stock information, or some other metadata to indicate the failure.

Without this circuit breaker, the inventory service failing could completely take down the catalog service, even though the catalog service is functioning properly. If we think back to Chapter 6 and our goal of embracing eventual consistency, the idea of building our systems around the idea that the tripped circuit breaker will *eventually* go back to normal shouldn't scare us.

As Fowler illustrates in his pseudocode, we usually set up a circuit breaker as a wrapper around the client that communicates with the backing service. It is within this wrapper that the state of the circuit (open/bad, closed/good) is maintained, as well as the metadata identifying the conditions under which the circuit should be tripped. You can see this illustrated in his definition of the `state` variable:

```
def state
  (@failure_count >= @failure_threshold) ? :open : :closed
end
```

As with so many of the other common problems we encounter when building microservice ecosystems, there is a Netflix OSS solution for this. This product is called Hystrix. You can find an overview of the Hystrix product on Netflix's GitHub wiki (*https://github.com/Netflix/Hystrix/wiki*).

Netflix's implementation is only for Java, but there are plenty of libraries available for you to evaluate if you think circuit breakers are what you need. A library worth looking at is Polly (*https://github.com/App-vNext/Polly*). Polly provides a very elegant, fluent syntax for declaring policies for retries, timeouts, circuit breakers, and more.

Here's a sample of Polly's declarative circuit breaker syntax taken from its documentation:

```
Policy
    .Handle<DivideByZeroException>()
    .CircuitBreaker(2, TimeSpan.FromMinutes(1));

Action<Exception, TimeSpan> onBreak = (exception, timespan) =>
    { ... };
Action onReset = () => { ... };
CircuitBreakerPolicy breaker = Policy
    .Handle<DivideByZeroException>()
    .CircuitBreaker(2, TimeSpan.FromMinutes(1), onBreak, onReset);
```

If Polly seems a little heavy-handed or seems to solve too many problems for you, there are some other lightweight alternatives available on GitHub that can be found with a quick search for "C# circuit breaker."

The one piece of advice I want to impart here is that you should spend the bulk of your time figuring out *if* you need circuit breakers, not *which* implementation you need. Circuit breakers come with their own added complexity and maintenance costs, and can often increase the amount of nested synchronous calls in a design because their presence can lull developers and architects into a false sense of security.

Eliminating the Synchronous Composite Pattern

The most important decision to make about circuit breakers or composite services isn't how to implement them, but whether we need them at all. Obviously, we don't always live in the land of unicorns, rainbows, and ideal service architectures. However, if we spend a little time analyzing our problems and potential solutions, looking for ways around common pitfalls, we might be able to avoid service composition.

Let's take a look at the example we've been using: the catalog and inventory services. Do we *really* need to know the exact, real-time inventory status of any product at all times? If we take a look at how frequently that data might change, then we realize that we probably don't need to compose these services the way we have.

What if the inventory service updated a cache every time a significant change occurred in the status of an item? In this scenario, the catalog service doesn't need to make a synchronous call to the inventory service; it can just query the cache keyed by product ID. If there's no cache data, then we can try and call the inventory service. If the inventory service fails temporarily, then the worst-case scenario is the catalog service will report the *last known* inventory status. When the inventory service recovers, it can refresh the cache accordingly.

With this pattern, we don't need to implement any retry logic, and we don't need to build in exponential back-off polling or use a heavyweight circuit breaker framework. Instead, we take advantage of the fact that in this case, the expectations of consumers can be met with a simpler, asynchronous solution.

This won't always be the case, and complexity is always lurking around the corner. The moral of the story here is to always *question complexity*. Every time something looks complicated, or seems as though it adds a weakness or a critical point of failure to your architecture, reexamine the needs that drove you to that design and see if there's something simpler and less tightly coupled that can solve the same problem.

What Next?

First and foremost, *question everything*. Take every piece of advice and every line of code you've seen in this book and put it to the test. Start writing your own services, build incredible applications, and improve upon everything you found here. If there are ways to improve this book's code samples, submit a pull request to the GitHub repositories. If you find something wrong with .NET Core itself, submit a pull request. Everyone can contribute now.

This book is a starting point. Hopefully it's provided you with inspiration and enough technical foundation to build powerful, elastically scalable, cross-platform microservices with C# and .NET Core.

If you build something incredible with .NET Core, share it. Write blog posts, write books, present at user groups and conferences, go on a tweetstorm about how amazing it is that you can build microservices in C# on your Mac, or go on an epic rant about how .NET Core falls short of your expectations and then suggest ways to fix it.

.NET Core is definitely a 1.0 product, and it is still in its infancy. It needs advocates and critics, people who will use it in production and find real ways to improve and solidify it to make it a dominant platform for building cloud-native microservices.

Index

About the Author

Kevin Hoffman has been programming since he was 10 years old, when he was left alone with a rebuilt Commodore VIC-20 and a BASIC programming manual. Ever since then, he has been addicted to emerging technologies, languages, and platforms.

He has written code for just about every industry, including biometric security, waste management, guidance systems for consumer-grade drones, financial services, and a bunch more. He's written over a dozen books on computer programming and has presented at a number of user groups and conferences, including Apple's WWDC and ScalaDays.

These days Kevin teaches development teams how to migrate and modernize their enterprise applications to thrive in the cloud with the latest cloud-native patterns, practices, and technology. Kevin is currently building cloud-native applications, patterns, and practices for Capital One.

Colophon

The animals on the cover of *Building Microservices with ASP.Net Core* are various birds of the tit family (*Paridae*). These birds can be found throughout Africa and the Northern Hemisphere. All tits are small, social, and prefer woodland environments where they can nest in tree cavities.

The great tit (*Parus major*) is a fairly colorful bird with white plumage on its cheeks surrounded by black on the rest of the head and neck. Upper plumage is a dirty green, while the undersides are of a more yellow tint. Like most tits, the great tit's diet consists mainly of insects. But when the insects become scarce in the winter months, the great tit has been known to consume smaller hibernating bats.

The blue tit (*Cyanistes caeruleus*) is even more colorful than the great tit, with more shades of blue, yellow, white, and streaks of black in plumage. They are, on average, 4 to 5 inches in length, with a wingspan of about 7 inches. Also known as the Eurasian tit, these birds can be found in Europe and Asia, and have a number of subspecies within the family.

The crested tit (*Lophophanes cristatus*) is less colorful than its previously mentioned relatives, but has distinctive facial plumage and crest (hence its name). The head is mostly white, with broken pieces of black through the forehead and crest. The chin is completely black. The upper body is of a green olive color, sides are a shade of yellow, and undersides are white.

The willow tit (*Poecile montanus*) is much more muted in colors than the previously mentioned tits. The top half of its head is completely black, while the cheeks and neck are white (but back to black on its chin). Also found in Europe and northern Asia, the willow tit's body colors vary in shading. Some appear to have wing plumage of a dark brown color, with lighter beige undersides, while others have more gray wings and white undersides. These birds are often mistaken for marsh tits, which have a very similar appearance.

The coal tit (*Periparus ater*) is found in parts of Europe, Asia, and northern Africa. Like many of the tits already mentioned, the coal tit's head is mostly black, with the back of the neck and cheeks being of white plumage. Undersides are shades of white, flanked by a pale yellow-brown coloring. These colorings and overall appearances vary through the many subspecies of coal tits.

Many of the animals on O'Reilly covers are endangered; all of them are important to the world. To learn more about how you can help, go to *animals.oreilly.com*.

The cover image is from *Wood's Natural History*. The cover fonts are URW Typewriter and Guardian Sans. The text font is Adobe Minion Pro; the heading font is Adobe Myriad Condensed; and the code font is Dalton Maag's Ubuntu Mono.

Learn from experts.
Find the answers you need.

Sign up for a **10-day free trial** to get **unlimited access** to all of the content on Safari, including Learning Paths, interactive tutorials, and curated playlists that draw from thousands of ebooks and training videos on a wide range of topics, including data, design, DevOps, management, business—and much more.

Start your free trial at:
oreilly.com/safari

(No credit card required.)

©2016 O'Reilly Media, Inc. O'Reilly is a registered trademark of O'Reilly Media, Inc. D2565

Milton Keynes UK
Ingram Content Group UK Ltd.
UKHW050141090524
442424UK00008B/396